MANAGING REDUNDANCY

Alan Fowler has worked widely in both the private and public sectors, with personnel appointments in four industries and two local authorities. He is now a freelance consultant, a director of Personnel Publications Ltd, and a member of the editorial board of *People Management*, the fortnightly journal of the IPD. He writes extensively on personnel issues, with regular articles in *People Management* and the *Local Government Chronicle*. His books for the IPD include *The Disciplinary Interview* (1996) and *Negotiating, Persuading and Influencing* (1995), both in the Management Shapers series; *Negotiation Skills and Strategies* (second edition 1996); *Get More – and More Results – from Your People* (1998); *Get More – and More Value – from Your People* (1998); and *Induction* (1999) in the Good Practice series. All these titles are available from the IPD.

The Institute of Personnel and Development is the leading publisher of books and reports for personnel and training professionals, students, and for all those concerned with the effective management and development of people at work. For details of all our titles, please contact the Publishing Department:

tel. 020-8263 3387
fax 020-8263 3850
e-mail publish@ipd.co.uk
The catalogue of all IPD titles can be viewed on the IPD website:
www.ipd.co.uk

MANAGING REDUNDANCY

Alan Fowler

INSTITUTE OF PERSONNEL AND DEVELOPMENT

The first edition of this book was published as *Redundancy* by the
Institute of Personnel Management 1993 (ISBN 0 85292 497 6).

This second edition first published by the Institute of
Personnel and Development 1999.

Design by Paperweight
Typeset by The Comp-Room, Aylesbury
Printed in Great Britain by
The Cromwell Press, Trowbridge, Wiltshire

British Library Cataloguing in Publication Data
A catalogue record for this book is available from the
British Library

ISBN 0-85292-819-X

The views expressed in this book are the author's own, and
may not necessarily reflect those of the IPD.

**INSTITUTE OF PERSONNEL
AND DEVELOPMENT**

IPD House, Camp Road, London SW19 4UX
Tel: 020-8971 9000   Fax: 020-8263 3333
Registered office as above. Registered Charity No. 1038333
A company limited by guarantee. Registered in England No. 2931892

CONTENTS

LIST OF ABBREVIATIONS

ACAS	Advisory, Conciliation and Arbitration Service
CA	Court of Appeal
CV	Curriculum vitae
DTI	Department of Trade and Industry
EAT	Employment Appeal Tribunal
ECJ	European Court of Justice
ERA	Employment Rights Act 1996
ETO	Economic, technical or organisational (reason)
IDS	Incomes Data Services
IIP	Investors in People
IRLR	Industrial Relations Law Reports
LIFO	Last in, first out
NI	National Insurance
NVQ	National Vocational Qualification
PAYE	Pay As You Earn
TEC	Training and Enterprise Council
TULR(C)A	Trade Union and Labour Relations (Consolidation) Act
TUPE	Transfer of Undertakings (Protection of Employment) Regulations 1981

LIST OF STATUTES AND REGULATIONS

Collective Redundancies and Transfer of Undertakings (Protection of Employment) (Amendments) Regulations 1995
Disability Discrimination Act 1995
Employment Rights Act 1996
Insolvency Act 1986
National Minimum Wage Act 1998
Public Interest Disclosure Act 1998
Race Relations Act 1976
Redundancy Payments Act 1965
Sex Discrimination Act 1975
Trade Union and Labour Relations (Consolidation) Act 1992
Trade Union Reform and Employment Rights Act 1993
Transfer of Undertakings (Protection of Employment) Regulations 1981
Wages Act 1986

1 INTRODUCTION

In today's volatile world of work, the survival and success of most organisations depend on their ability to adopt a strategy of continual adaptation in response to the threats and opportunities of the fast-moving external environment. Technological developments, global competition, the emergence of new markets, demographic and political change – such factors as these mean that few organisations can escape the need to make frequent adjustments to the way they are structured, their systems and processes, their relationships with stakeholders and their links with other organisations with which they may form working partnerships.

The effective planning and implementation of these developments are crucially influenced by how well the people-management issues are handled, particularly when changes are needed to the size or composition of a workforce. All aspects of people management are involved, including recruitment, selection, training, teambuilding, leadership and communication, and most of these topics are the subject of a considerable academic and professional literature. But there is one effect of organisational change that, although it has a major impact on employee morale and can carry substantial cost, has received relatively little attention in the management literature – redundancy. The purpose of this book is, consequently, to suggest how redundancy may best be managed, and to do so by recognising that there are two aspects to consider – good practice from a people-management viewpoint and the legal context in which this must be set.

These two aspects are, of course, related. Redundancy legislation and the way it is interpreted by the tribunals and courts often appear highly complex in the legal minutiae, but underlying the detail is a broad concept of fairness. Good management practice must include an understanding of the law and full compliance with its detailed provisions, but it has a wider concern that accepts these provisions as setting only the minimum standards that form a basis for best practice. In addition, a starting-point for any organisation that wishes to manage redundancy well is to consider what it can do to prevent redundancy occurring – or, if it occurs, to minimise its impact. Redundancy avoidance is as much an element of redundancy management as the processing of the termination of employment of people who have become surplus to the organisation's requirements.

Chapters 2 and 3 therefore address this aspect in its two main forms – strategic or long-term human resourcing strategies which contribute to the development of an adaptable organisation better able to achieve change without redundancy; and operational or short-term measures to reduce the impact of redundancy if this becomes unavoidable.

In considering the management of actual redundancies, it is essential to understand the legal context. Statute and case-law on the subject are very extensive, and falling foul of many of the detailed legal provisions can be very expensive. Organisations need to have a sound set of redundancy policies and procedures, and although these will address matters outside and beyond the strict legal requirements, they must incorporate all the principles and practices set out in the relevant statutes and defined by the courts in leading cases. It is also of critical importance that managers handling redundancy comply with their organisations' procedures and understand the legal risks of not doing so. To take just one example, treating a dismissal as a disciplinary matter when the courts would interpret this as redundancy – or vice versa – may well result in a large-scale compensation award. Chapter 4 consequently looks at the legal definition of redundancy, whereas Chapters 5 to 10 also set the management of the various aspects of redundancy within the relevant legal context.

Although the book goes into some detail about the legal aspects, the aim has been to provide explanations in lay, rather than legal, terms. There are therefore very few direct quotations from the various statutes and statutory regulations and illustrative case-law has been heavily summarised. Readers wishing to study the legal aspects in more detail should refer to the publications listed at the end of the book.

The book concludes (in Chapter 11) with another aspect of redundancy management which, like redundancy avoidance, is not significantly influenced by legal considerations. The only action that the law prescribes, once the fairness of an individual redundancy has been established, is a compensation payment at a relatively low level. Good management recognises, however, that redundancy is a traumatic event for those who lose their jobs and a cause of worry and uncertainty for the survivors. Far more can be done to help people cope than simply paying the statutory lump sum, and the good employer accepts a responsibility both for providing a much wider range of assistance to the redundant employees and for taking action to maintain the morale and commitment of those who remain.

Redundancy is not a subject that excites the innovative personnel professional or the entrepreneurial manager. It may also seem at times to be dominated by complicated legal provisions. In reality, the development of redundancy avoidance strategies and the effective management of redundancy requires a blend of humanity, efficiency and understanding of the law which constitutes a major test of managerial competence. Managing a redundancy situation will never be an enjoyable experience, but to do so well – knowing that the people affected and their surviving colleagues accept that it has been unavoidable and handled fairly and sensitively – can at least be the source of some professional satisfaction. The purpose of this book is to help readers who may have to cope with redundancy face this test with a sound knowledge of the issues involved and the confidence to put this knowledge to good practical effect.

2 AVOIDING REDUNDANCY: THE STRATEGIC APPROACH

The ideal redundancy objective is to manage the organisation's human resource requirements in such a way that the need for redundancy never arises. Like most ideals, this is rarely attainable and no organisation can ever be wholly confident that circumstances will not occur in which its number or type of employees exceeds its need or ability to employ them. Nevertheless, realism about the difficulty of totally avoiding redundancy in no way detracts from the desirability of doing everything possible to minimise its possible incidence. This is not a simple matter of making declarations of intent. Indeed, some organisations that committed themselves to 'no redundancy' policy statements and collective agreements before the 1990 recession, without giving adequate consideration to the many measures necessary to reduce the possibility of redundancy, later found themselves in the damaging position of having to dismiss employees in breach of their own policies and agreements.

There are two aspects to redundancy avoidance – long-term or strategic, dealt with in this chapter, and short-term or operational, as discussed in Chapter 3. The main difference is that long-term action can be put in place before anything approaching a redundancy situation occurs, whereas short-term action is taken to avoid or minimise actual or imminent redundancies. The key feature of long-term measures is planning. As the Institute of Personnel and Development says in its *Guide on Redundancy*:

The IPD expects its members to encourage their organisations to take all reasonable steps to avoid the necessity of redundancies, and to develop planning and employment strategies which will enable their organisations to deal with short-term fluctuations in labour requirements. Even the most carefully handled redundancies are likely to result in a negative organisational culture and it therefore makes sense that redundancy is always viewed as a measure of last resort.

The identification or forecast of anticipated employee surpluses, although important, is not the whole planning story. A normal feature of any form of planning is that the out-turn in reality usually differs (at least in part) from the planning forecasts. In addition, in today's fast-moving and complex economic scene, it has become increasingly difficult to forecast major events – such as an increase in interest rates or a take-over bid – which can so readily throw a business off its planned course. The only certainty is change itself. Planning must therefore include measures to achieve flexibility of response to the unexpected, because it is the inflexible organisation that is most vulnerable in the face of change and therefore most likely to be forced into making redundancy dismissals.

Forecasting and flexibility

The two main aspects of planning to avoid redundancy are therefore forecasting and flexibility, and these in turn can be sub-divided into several elements, each of which is considered in turn in this chapter:

Forecasting   The business planning context
Human resource planning
Redundancy policies and collective agreements

Flexibility   Organisational factors
Job and work flexibility
Resourcing flexibility
Flexibility of conditions of employment

The importance of all these factors can be illustrated by considering the characteristics of an organisation that would be most at risk of having to effect redundancies:

☐ It would have made no assessments of the likely trends affecting the viability of the business. Its decisions will therefore be reactive, often resulting in crisis-management measures – including making sudden changes in the constitution and size of the workforce.

☐ It would have no clear business objectives, values or standards. Without this vision it will not be able to take long-term action to ensure the training and development of its people to meet future business needs. When changes become necessary in the type and mix of employee skills, it will consequently tend to make employees with old skills redundant and acquire the necessary new skills through recruitment.

☐ It would not have analysed the age and service profiles of its workforce, nor maintained statistics of the level and trends of employee turnover. Faced with a need to change the nature or size of its workforce, it will find difficulty in forecasting the effect of natural wastage, and may suddenly discover an imbalance in the age distribution of its staff which makes measures such as voluntary early retirement relatively ineffective.

☐ It would probably have a complex organisational hierarchy and a rigid and centralised management system. The risk of managerial redundancies will be greater than in a simpler organisational structure, while the centralised nature of its management system will inhibit rapid operational adjustments.

☐ Jobs would be very closely defined, with a multiplicity of work demarcations. This will inhibit the transfer of employees from job to job to meet changing operational pressures. Also, by institutionalising a large number of different 'particular kinds' of work, there will be an increased risk of claims for redundancy compensation from employees unable or unwilling to accept job transfers.

☐ Almost all its workforce would be permanent, full-time employees, with little or no use being made of part-timers, temporary and fixed-term contracts, or external contractors. There will consequently be very limited scope for varying the size of the workforce to reflect fluctuations in the level of the organisation's activities – other than by redundancy or recruitment.

☐ It would operate a complicated and very detailed set of conditions of employment, in which changes in working time or in job duties are difficult or costly to introduce, and require centralised approval. Although changes in employment conditions do not directly cause redundancy, inflexibility in such matters as overtime, shift patterns and payment systems will all restrict the organisation's ability to reorganise how work is done – and so will have an indirect but adverse effect on its ability to avoid redundancies.

☐ It will not have concluded any redundancy agreements with its trade unions, with the result that when redundancies occur, there is immediate disagreement as to how these should be handled.

Hopefully, there are now few organisations that are characterised by all these features, although many could be found until the late 1980s among public-sector bureaucracies. This was no accident, because these characteristics are very much those of organisations that have not been exposed to the risks and uncertainties of the commercial world and are concerned more with the maintenance of existing functions than with innovation and change. It would be optimistic, however, to claim that the majority of private-sector organisations were free of every one of these symptoms of rigidity.

Business planning

Planning to avoid redundancy cannot occur in a vacuum, nor can the whole planning process be focused solely on this one objective. The basis of effective redundancy avoidance lies in the organisation's business plan – its analysis of its current and targeted market position and the resources and skills it needs to achieve its business objectives. It is worth commenting that although the concept of business planning has obviously been developed in the private sector, many of the principles and processes involved have now been adopted and adapted by Civil Service agencies, health authorities, schools and local authorities. Any organisation, private or public, needs to take stock of what it is doing, the external trends (including threats and opportunities) for which it should develop action plans, and its strategic and operational objectives.

Aspects of business planning that have particular relevance to the assessment of the possibility of redundancies are:

☐ What is planned regarding the size of the business? Is it expected to expand, contract, or remain relatively stable in size?

☐ If expansion is planned – on what basis? Is this to be a general growth across all business activities, or is it to be concentrated on one or more particular aspects?

☐ Are changes planned in the nature of the business, such as increased specialisation, or the launch of new products or services?

☐ Do any of the plans involve changes to business or unit locations?

☐ Are there any plans to change qualitative or cultural aspects of the business, such as going up-market with products, or placing greater emphasis on customer service, or introducing a total quality management programme?

☐ What external trends are expected – economic, technological, statutory – that will necessitate change in the scope of the business or how it operates?

These kinds of issue generate many of the conditions in which an organisation may experience surpluses or shortfalls in the workforce, both quantitative and qualitative.

Human resource planning

Human resource planning is a broader concept than traditional manpower planning which tended to concentrate on statistical forecasting of the size of the workforce. The manpower planner of the 1960s and 1970s produced a mathematical model of the organisation, computerised when the numbers were large, and calculated the inflow, outflow and net result of various business scenarios, incorporating statistical data about employee turnover and projected labour availability. The emphasis was on projections of labour demand and supply, often without much thought to alternative resourcing or organisational strategies, or to non-quantitative factors.

Human resource planning includes this type of statistical analysis, but has several important additional features:

☐ It is built into the business planning process, rather than being treated as a separate and specialist function. As a result, human resource issues and projections may influence the business plan – instead of business decisions being made first and their personnel implications being left to the personnel manager to deal with later. For example, the timing of an expansion plan may well be determined by estimates of the volume, cost and duration of necessary retraining programmes. Or initial proposals about the scope and pace of a relocation plan may be modified by assessments of staff wastage rates and the costs of possible redundancies.

☐ It is concerned as much (if not more) with the design, implementation and monitoring of action plans as with statistical forecasting and analysis. Conventional manpower planning often stopped at the end of the analysis phase, the specialist planner handing over the statistical projections to line management who may or may not have taken much notice of the personnel implications.

☐ Qualitative factors are given as much attention as quantitative data. Thus, if the business plan calls for a greater emphasis on quality or customer care, human resource planning will assess and suggest the action needed in terms of training, job design, employee consultation and the like in order to achieve the necessary cultural change. Plans to achieve greater flexibility – discussed in the next sections of this chapter – provide further examples both of the qualitative aspects of human resource planning and of its proactive role in developing action plans to meet the needs of the business.

In relation to redundancy avoidance, it is for the human resource function to explain why this is important and to evolve and argue for the practical measures that need to be taken. Three types of information and analysis are involved:

☐ the business-planning data about such issues as technological and market trends, as outlined earlier in this chapter; and the options under consideration for the development of the organisation in the light of these trends

□ external influences on the organisation's human resourcing
  capability, particularly
  – demographic change
  – the availability of or competition for the skills the organ-
    isation will need
  – UK and EU employment-related legislation, eg the statu-
    tory requirement to consult with trade unions or
    employee representatives on measures to avoid redun-
    dancy
□ the characteristics and constitution of the current workforce, with particular reference to
  – age and gender profiles
  – stability and turnover levels and trends
  – the stock of skills and competencies
  – organisation structures and the design of jobs
  – the extent of other than conventional full-time employ-
    ment (eg part-timers, temporary staff, contractors).

From a review of all these factors one can draw indicators of the
changes to the organisation's workforce that will be needed to
meet the various business options being considered. Assuming,
as is likely, that there are indications of a mis-match between
current and future requirements, three alternative courses of
action are open:

□ Go ahead with the most favoured business plan, maintain
  current organisational and personnel policies, and plan to
  meet the indicated surpluses or shortfalls in the human
  resource by redundancy or recruitment. If redundancy is indicated, the aim can be to reduce its impact by the short-term
  measures discussed in Chapter 3.
□ Modify the business plan to minimise any major redundancy
  or recruitment problems that may be indicated.
□ Plan and implement long-term and permanent changes to
  current human resourcing strategies and employment practices in order to enable the business to achieve its preferred
  business objectives without experiencing the problems with
  shortfalls or surpluses that would otherwise occur.

Most of the long-term measures to avoid redundancy come
under the heading of flexibility, as discussed in the following

sections of this chapter, and their relevance varies according to the circumstances of any given organisation at a particular point in time. But there are two issues of general significance to most organisations:

☐ *training*: the extent to which employees' skills and competences are under continuous development, not just for the work that each employee does now, but for work to which they may be transferred or for which a future demand can be forecast. The more versatile the workforce, the less likely it is that employees will have to be made redundant when the requirement for their current skills diminishes or ceases and is replaced by a need for new skills. The approach that will deliver this outcome is very much in line with the principles of Investors in People (IIP). The IIP standard emphasises that training and development should be integrated with the organisation's business plan, applied to all employees, and be periodically updated to reflect changing business and operational needs. Most IIP employers are likely to be in better shape to respond to these changing needs without having to effect redundancies than organisations with either little training activity or training limited to a narrow range of conventional skills.

☐ *retirement*: the organisation's retirement and pension policies and provisions that can influence the scale of natural wastage. For example, to extend the normal retiring age from 60 to, say, 63 will reduce turnover to some extent in a predominantly female workforce and increase wastage if the same age is introduced for a largely male workforce that has been retiring at 65. A less rigid approach than adopting a single fixed age for retirement may be even more effective as one of the flexibility measures discussed below.

Organisational flexibility

Many organisations are structured along functional or specialist lines. This may reflect professional groupings such as engineering or accountancy or be linked to different stages in a work process – such as machining, assembly and inspection. Either way, there is a rigidity about this type of organisation that inhibits other than marginal change. It may also reinforce a sense of identity with, and loyalty to, the particular profession or occupation rather than to the organisation as a whole.

This can work against the long-term interests of the organisation by limiting its ability to adapt to change, and against the job security interests of employees by restricting their knowledge and skills within relatively narrow boundaries. If, for example, the introduction of modern quality management involves machine operators taking responsibility for the quality-checking of their own output, many of the existing inspectors may have no other skills or experience and so be unable to transfer to other work. For them, a change of management practice may then mean redundancy, even if the organisation as a whole is expanding. There is also an attitudinal aspect, displaced employees from one specialist section displaying reluctance to move to other sections which they perceive as alien (or lower in status) in professional or occupational terms.

There may, of course, be sound technological or other reasons for maintaining this traditional form of organisation. If so, attention will have to be paid to other ways of injecting flexibility into the system. But if there is no practical bar to organisational change, the possible incidence of redundancy can certainly be reduced by grouping employees not by profession or function but by product or service. This will involve multi-disciplinary teams in the professional sector, and multi-skilled work groups in manufacturing or service industries. There are, of course, more important reasons for adopting such working patterns than the avoidance of redundancy – but these lie outside the scope of this book. Suffice it to say that such factors as the reduction of supervisory expenditure, the generation of a greater sense of employee commitment, higher quality and improved customer service have all been quoted as benefits of multi-functional teamworking.

In addition to functional inflexibility there may also be complexity and rigidity within the supervisory and managerial hierarchy. Managerial work may be finely differentiated, with numerous hierarchical levels. Each manager or supervisor then has responsibility for a relatively limited range of functions. When circumstances force a change in the distribution or nature of the organisation's various activities, individual managers and supervisors quickly become displaced, particularly in the middle sector between top management and first-line supervision. Many managerial redundancies during the past 10 or 15 years have resulted from 'de-layering', when organisations have decided their hierarchies have become too complex and have then stripped out entire management or supervisory levels. Rather than having to mount a traumatic exercise of this kind, it is better – if time allows – to move from a conventionally complex management structure to a slimmer, flatter system on a planned but evolutionary basis, taking advantage of every managerial retirement or resignation to broaden the remaining managers' jobs and reduce the number of levels in the hierarchy.

Job flexibility

Organisational flexibility is primarily about how jobs are grouped. Job flexibility is concerned with the design or content of individual jobs. These two issues tend to be linked, as it is often a feature of a rigid organisational structure that individual jobs within it are narrowly defined, each employee concerned with just one small element in a broader work process, and unable to complete a whole transaction.

The origins of this fractured system lie in the so-called 'scientific management' movement of the 1930s and 1940s, expounded in the writings of authors such as F W Taylor and Max Weber, and applied and developed in mass-production industries, particularly motor-manufacturing in the USA. Taylor showed that on a strict time-and-motion study basis, the most efficient way to organise any repetitive work process was to break it down into its smallest component parts and then train workers to achieve very high rates of performance in the completion of these individual and often minute tasks. Weber applied similar thinking to administrative and managerial work, and the key word in both cases was *specialisation*.

The complex and bureaucratic work systems that were widely developed on the basis of these theories could be justified as efficient in two sets of circumstances: where little or no attention was paid to employee commitment or development; and where little regard was given either to the probability of continual change or to how major changes in technology, products and services could be achieved without adverse human-resource implications. The approach suited a hire-and-fire employment philosophy but became increasingly unsatisfactory as new technology made it possible to computerise or automate simple repetitive tasks. Organisations also became more aware of the very limited extent to which they had been utilising the real potential within their workforces, while employment legislation brought significant costs to casual hiring and firing.

As a consequence, the later 1980s and early 1990s saw many organisations embarking on programmes of job enlargement and multi-skilling. Ford UK reduced its number of job categories from 516 in 1986 to 45 in 1988, while a similar process of grouping previously separate specialisms together to construct more rounded jobs has been implemented by many organisations in all economic sectors. As noted earlier, strategies of these kinds are not adopted solely to reduce the likelihood of redundancies, but they make a major contribution to this aim. Employees who are able to handle a range of tasks, instead of being expert in only one, obviously find it far easier to adapt to changes in working methods or to move from one function in the organisation to another as job requirements fluctuate.

Organisational and job flexibility demand considerable managerial effort in their planning and implementation. The organisation needs to ensure that new patterns of working are cost-effective in both the immediate and longer term. Furthermore, to equip employees with the skills to undertake broader job roles requires a co-ordinated and continuous training programme. Modular training is the normal approach, employees building up their stock of skills over time and having refresher and updating training to maintain standards and keep abreast of technological and other developments.

Flexibility in human resourcing

There is a wider issue that can make an even greater contribution to the avoidance of redundancy – flexibility in the organisation's human resourcing. The traditional organisation got all its work done by a workforce of full-time employees. This caused no problems while the volume of work and the number of employees required remained static or changed only slowly. Drip-feed recruitment satisfied modest expansion requirements, whereas unforced retirements and resignations enabled painless though minor reductions to be made in the size of the workforce.

But with the pace of change having quickened, organisations resourced in this way have experienced considerable difficulty in responding to faster and larger fluctuations in their requirements for employees. At one time, the answer to this problem was to staff for an expected average volume of work, meeting upwards fluctuations by overtime and using short-time working or lay-offs to cope with sudden reductions. This method may still suffice for some organisations, though the high costs of overtime and the complexity of legislation governing lay-offs and guarantee payments (see Chapter 8) raise questions about its cost-effectiveness.

A more fundamental solution is the concept of the core and periphery organisation, of which Charles Handy has been a major exponent. In essence, this suggests the use of three forms of resourcing:

☐ a relatively small central core of highly skilled employees on direct, permanent contracts, with the size of this workforce set at close to the minimum expected level of requirement

☐ a larger group of secondary employees, on terms such as fixed-term and temporary contracts which make it possible (subject to some legal constraints) to change their number relatively quickly and without incurring redundancy costs

☐ an outer ring of outworkers of various kinds (not employees) such as agency staff, self-employed freelance workers, contractors and consultants. Their use can be changed even more rapidly than that of the secondary employees.

There is no doubt that this concept provides a high degree of job security to the core employees, with the organisation's redundancy risks considerably reduced. Clearly, it does not guard against business failure, but it does provide a system that has far more flexibility in its response to large or sudden business fluctuations than the conventionally resourced organisation.

There are arguments for and against this concept which have nothing to do with redundancy issues – in particular, doubts have been raised about the social effects of the possible creation of a two-class employment system: highly paid, protected core workers and poorly rewarded and insecure secondary employees. These arguments lie outside the scope of this book. Here, three points can be made that are redundancy-related:

- ☐ Any move away from the conventional use of only direct, permanent employees will contribute to a redundancy avoidance policy. To that extent, the core/periphery concept has much to commend it.

- ☐ A cautionary note must be sounded, however, about any idea that part-time working should form a major element of the secondary group of employees. EU and related UK legislation makes less favourable terms for part-timers either directly unlawful, or indirectly discriminatory if – as is often the case – a higher proportion of part-time than full-time employees are women.

- ☐ It must not be assumed that all redundancy costs can readily be avoided simply by the use of temporary or fixed-term contracts. There are circumstances (described in the next chapter) in which so-called temporary employees may acquire redundancy rights, and the non-renewal of a fixed-term contract may also in some cases be interpreted in legal terms as a redundancy dismissal. There may also be penalty clauses for the early termination of commercial and consultancy contracts.

Flexible conditions of employment

The introduction of flexibility into organisations and jobs may be inhibited if conditions of employment are not also revised to support this flexibility. Changes in an employee's duties may be restricted by complex job-grading systems in which even very minor alterations to a detailed schedule of work activities result in claims for regrading. Whether an employee is contractually bound to accept a locational move or a transfer to other work may also be central to a redundancy decision. From the viewpoint of a redundancy avoidance policy, there are several key elements of the employment package where flexibility is of most significance.

Contractual duties

The question as to whether redundancy has occurred may in some cases be dependent on an assessment of what the employee has been required to do under the contract of employment, and where he or she has been required to work. Within reason, therefore, there is an advantage in contracts of employment avoiding too specific a schedule of work duties or limiting the job location to one fixed site. A common cause of difficulty is the issue of a detailed job description, which employees often assume forms an element in the contract of employment – though in reality, job descriptions are only treated by the courts as contractual if they have been expressly incorporated into the contract. If the job description is limited to a list of the duties the employee is initially required to perform, it may be a source of dispute about the employer's right to make later changes to these duties. One result may be the employee resigning and then claiming constructive dismissal for redundancy. There are several ways of avoiding this problem:

□ Make it clear that the job description is not contractual by prefacing it with a statement to the effect that: 'This job description is a guide to the duties you will be expected to perform immediately on your appointment. It is not part of your contract of employment, and your duties may well be changed from time to time to meet changes in the company's requirements.'

□ Whether or not the job description is contractual, issue only a very short outline of the general nature of the work, plus a statement that: 'Your detailed duties, which may change from time to time, will be explained to you by your supervisor.'

□ Again, whether or not the job description is contractual, conclude the list of duties within the job description with a clause along the lines: 'such other duties as the company may reasonably require from time to time'.

Contractual documents may need to set out the position regarding locational mobility. If the organisation operates on more than one site, or if there is any likelihood of a move to a new location, a decision is needed as to whether all or some employees (and, if so, which) should be required contractually to accept a change of work location. Letters of appointment, which normally have contractual status, may need to include phrases saying something like:

Initially you will be employed in the . . . department at . . . but you may be required to transfer to any other of the company's departments or work locations.

Note that this particular phrase covers inter-departmental transfers within the same location as well as locational moves. In relation to the latter, it is good employment practice to add something to the effect that:

> You will be given reasonable notice of any such move and the company also provides relocation assistance in these circumstances.

It should be noted, however, that the courts are unlikely to accept the validity of open-ended mobility clauses in cases where it is obviously unreasonable to enforce them, or in cases where there is evidence that although a mobility clause exists, in practice and over a lengthy period mobility has never been required.

Working times

A rigid adherence to a Monday to Friday, 8 or 9am to 5pm work-time schedule may well restrict the organisation's ability to make quick adjustments to meet changing customer requirements, either in volume terms or in types of service (eg equipment maintenance out of normal hours). This rigidity can contribute to a company losing its competitive edge and so heading towards failure and redundancies. Some work, too, has seasonal peaks and troughs, and the flexible organisation meets these by adopting flexibility in standard working hours. Finding work for displaced employees can also be eased if there is some choice in work schedules, particularly if job transfers involve additional home-to-work travel time, or difficulties in normal attendance times because of inadequate public transport. Among the flexibility measures to consider are:

☐ annual working hours contracts, with a requirement to complete a defined basic total of hours each year, but with a minimum of prescription about daily or weekly working times

☐ for seasonal work such as grounds maintenance, different basic weekly hours between summer and winter (eg 44 hours from April to September, and 36 hours from October to the following March)

☐ evening or weekend shifts – or other part-time arrangements which may involve a requirement to average, say, 18 hours per week within a range of 10 to 24 hours per week.

A related form of flexibility is to permit or arrange for employees to work either at home or on a mixed home/office basis. The emphasis then is on employees completing a required or satisfactory volume of work, relative to their pay, rather than meeting a requirement to be present for work for a defined number of hours. How much time the employee spends working at home is immaterial provided output targets are met. There is probably more scope in a redundancy situation to make adjustments to these output requirements than there is in a conventional working arrangement where hours of work might have formally to be cut. Home-based working may also contribute to the avoidance of redundancies resulting from locational moves.

Relocation schemes

The incidence of redundancy resulting from major locational moves can be reduced by schemes to assist employees in relocating. Such schemes may include:

☐ organised visits for employees and their families to the new location in advance of the move

☐ the provision of information and advice about such matters as children's schooling, the availability of jobs for spouses, recreational facilities and the like

☐ assistance with house sale and purchase, probably by using a specialist relocation agency

☐ the payment of relocation costs

☐ subsidies for extra travel costs.

A range of measures of these kinds can massively cut the potential redundancy costs when an organisation relocates but a large proportion of employees decide they are not able to move.

Retirement and pensions

Reference has already been made in relation to human resource planning of the implications for natural wastage of fixed retirement ages. More flexibility can be introduced by setting only a minimum retirement age for a normal pension, and permitting two variants:

☐ optional early retirement – though this involves reduced

pensions unless the organisation wishes to stimulate such retirement by offering pension enhancements (see Chapter 3 for short-term measures of this kind)

☐ optional later retirement – including a contractual clause reserving to the employer the right to require retirement at any time after the minimum age has been reached, but not specifying a final age. Extended service past the minimum age normally results in the accrual of additional pension benefit (within Inland Revenue limits).

Retirement schemes with these provisions can assist in achieving voluntary departures as well as enabling turnover to be increased or slowed to meet expected staff surpluses or shortfalls, depending on the use made of the employer's right to require retirement after the minimum age of, say, 60 or 62.

Involving the trade unions

Introducing various forms of flexibility within an organisation that has previously followed conventional employment practices requires a change of attitude among managers and employees if the changes are to be accepted and operated with commitment. In a unionised environment, it is clearly important to secure trade union agreement to any changes which overturn previously negotiated terms and conditions, and (as a minimum) to avoid outright union opposition to issues that although non-negotiable (such as changes to management structures), nevertheless have an impact on union members' working lives. Ideally, all changes would be fully explained, the unions' responses and reactions be given full consideration, and the final decisions receive positive union support.

The stereotyped union position is probably thought of as opposition to change, resistance to flexibility measures, and a preference for the detailed specification of precisely defined and standardised employment conditions. There is some truth in most stereotypes and an organisation planning for flexibility would do well to realise that attitudes of this kind – whether institutionalised through the trade unions or specific to individual employees – may well exist. But trade unions have another characteristic which can run counter to resistance to change – pragmatism in the face of reality. Trade unions are keenly concerned to protect their members against redundancy – more so than some managers. If the positive reasons for the measures described in this chapter are fully explained and discussed, and if the organisation is open with its analyses and forecasts of change, initial and understandable union caution can be converted to agreement and co-operation.

Redundancy policies and collective agreements

Because the possibility of redundancies becoming necessary can never be wholly avoided, it is advisable for any organisation to give thought as to how this situation would be handled if it arose. The principles to be followed and at least an outline of the procedure can then be endorsed as a formal policy – which would normally open with a commitment to take all possible steps to avoid redundancy. One of the benefits of having a defined redundancy policy is that managers throughout the organisation will then know what they are expected to do if a job becomes redundant. Consistency in the handling of individual redundancies across an organisation and the collaboration of managers in different units or functions in identifying alternative jobs are both important – in terms not only of good practice but also of compliance with principles established by case-law.

In a unionised environment, it is helpful for these principles and procedures to be incorporated in a collective agreement, and for this agreement to be produced at a time when there is no impending redundancy situation. It can be difficult to negotiate an agreement that strikes a fair balance between the ongoing needs of the organisation and the immediate needs of the employee in the midst of what may well be a business crisis. The value of having a redundancy agreement, in addition to ensuring the operation of a fair procedure, is that it should prevent the damaging and costly dispute that could otherwise arise if an unexpected redundancy situation occurred and it then became evident that the organisation and the trade union had very different views as to how it should be handled. The main elements in a redundancy agreement are normally:

☐ a commitment by the organisation to take all reasonable steps to avoid redundancy, or, if it becomes necessary, to minimise its impact

- a commitment by the organisation to effective consultation in the event of the possibility of redundancy and how such consultation would be effected
- a commitment by the trade union to co-operate in action to avoid or minimise redundancy
- agreed selection criteria for redundancy (see Chapter 6), and the procedure for notifying the trade union and the employees involved (see Chapter 7)
- details of redundancy compensation (see Chapter 9)
- details of any other assistance the organisation would provide to redundant employees (see Chapter 11).

Key points

- The ideal redundancy policy is one that results in no redundancies.
- Planning is the key to redundancy avoidance.
- The two main elements in effective planning to avoid redundancies are forecasting and flexibility.
- Organisations most at risk of experiencing redundancies are those that do not assess trends (market, technological, economic) and operate rigid systems of work, organisation and conditions of employment.
- The basis of effective redundancy avoidance planning is the organisation's business plan.
- The business plan should identify and assess all relevant trends, threats and opportunities; define the aims and standards of the business; and indicate necessary resourcing requirements.
- Human resource planning should be a component of, and should influence, the business plan.
- The human resource plan takes account of business data, assessments of external trends (eg in demography, employment legislation) and analyses of the characteristics of the workforce (eg age and stability profiles, skills stocks); produces forecasts of shortages and surpluses; and designs and monitors plans to meet business objectives cost-effectively – including the avoidance of the adverse effects of redundancy.
- In a unionised environment it is advisable to conclude a

collective agreement during a period in which no redundancies are occurring, setting out how a redundancy situation would be managed and the commitments of both parties to adhere to the procedures involved.

☐ Two issues of general relevance to the avoidance of redundancy within the context of general human resource planning are training, to produce a multi-skilled and adaptable workforce, and retirement and pension policies, which affect wastage rates.

☐ Organisational flexibility can contribute to an ability to adjust to change without having to effect redundancies. Two particular aspects are the disbandment of conventional professional or specialist organisational boundaries, and the introduction of flat or 'de-layered' management hierarchies.

☐ Flexibility in the design of jobs and work systems enables the organisation and the individual employee to adapt to change. Job enlargement and continuous occupational and professional development are essential features.

☐ Flexibility in staffing the organisation markedly reduces the possibility of redundancy. An important concept in this respect is that of core and peripheral resourcing – an inner core of skilled, permanent staff, supplemented by a secondary ring of employees on temporary and fixed-term contracts, and an outer ring of non-employed outworkers: agency staff, freelances, consultants and contractors.

☐ Care must be taken, however, to avoid treating part-timers less favourably than full-time employees.

☐ Flexible conditions of employment are needed to reinforce the other forms of flexibility. These include the use of mobility and flexibility clauses in contracts of employment; flexible working-time arrangements (eg annual hours contracts, seasonal variations in the standard working week, evening and weekend shifts); and variable pension and retirement arrangements.

☐ Redundancies resulting from major changes to work locations can be significantly reduced by comprehensive relocation schemes.

☐ In a unionised environment, the introduction and operation of flexible personnel policies benefits from their incorporation in collective agreements.

3 AVOIDING REDUNDANCY: THE OPERATIONAL APPROACH

Measures of the kind discussed in Chapter 2 make an organisation more adaptable to change and diminish the risk of its incurring redundancies, though no long-term measures can wholly guarantee that a redundancy situation will never arise. The sudden collapse of a major business customer, an escalation of interest rates, the impact of a takeover – these are all events that may be of a scale and rapidity that even the most flexible of organisations cannot absorb without making previously unplanned workforce reductions. However, this need not always result in enforced redundancy dismissals, because there are many short-term operational measures that can be taken to avoid or reduce such action, in particular:

- natural wastage and recruitment restrictions
- stopping or reducing overtime
- terminating the employment of non-permanent workers (temporary, casual, fixed-term contract, self-employed, agency employees)
- retraining and redeployment
- retirement measures
- volunteers for redundancy.

Short-time working and lay-offs can also be considered, although because of their legal complexity they are discussed separately (in Chapter 8).

Natural wastage

Natural wastage has become the common term for the effect of all forms of employee turnover other than redundancy dismissals. It therefore includes normal and ill-health retirements, deaths in service, resignations for all reasons other than impending redundancy, and a normal number of disciplinary dismissals. Most organisations faced with a need to effect staffing reductions attempt to meet at least part of these requirements by freezing or limiting recruitment for a period and allowing natural wastage to take effect. The extent to which this will solve a potential redundancy situation depends on several factors:

☐ *the scale and nature of the required reduction in the workforce*. Wastage is relevant only in the job categories from which reductions are required or in other jobs to which redundant employees might be transferred. In planning the use of natural wastage, it is therefore essential to know the actual and projected turnover rates for these particular categories, and not rely on statistics about the average turnover for the whole workforce. Two factors may limit the effectiveness of natural wastage: the need for large-scale reductions in a workforce with low turnover rates; or reductions being required of small numbers (even of single employees) in very specialised jobs. Waiting for the organisation's single surplus specialist to leave, when he or she is 20 years away from retirement age, is not an effective anti-redundancy measure.

☐ *the length of time available for wastage to have an effect*. The longer the time period, the larger the reduction. This gives further emphasis to the value of planning and forecasting and of an organisation taking control of its own situation. Putting off a decision to place restrictions on recruitment may result in compulsory redundancies which earlier action would have prevented. What is often overlooked in using natural wastage is that normal turnover will continue immediately after the target date for reductions to have been effected. It is not unknown for an organisation to ignore this and then have to begin recruitment in a particular area of work within a week or so of redundancies. Staff just made redundant may even be re-hired to fill these new vacancies caused by a quite normal number of resignations among the staff originally retained. Such incidents involve unnecessary expense in redundancy payments and may damage the organisation's reputation as an intelligent employer. Consequently, it is always useful to project the effect of natural wastage some way past the target date for workforce reductions and consider whether the redundancies originally planned might be reduced, to take account of likely wastage during this extended period.

☐ *the extent to which recruitment can be frozen without damaging the organisation*. The detailed effects of natural wastage cannot be forecast: which people will leave which jobs is something of a lottery – except for normal retirements. On a large scale, or over a long period, the non-replacement of every leaver can result in a serious distortion of the stock of skills and experience in the workforce. Organisations need to monitor the detailed nature of wastage very closely during a run-down period in case employees leave who represent losses of experience, knowledge or skills which need immediate replacement – even though overall reductions may still be necessary in the job category concerned. It may be unwise, therefore, to apply a total recruitment freeze, though this may require detailed and persuasive discussion with the trade unions. A phrase covering this point in some collective agreements on redundancy runs along the following lines.

> In the event of an expected redundancy situation, the company will make every possible use of natural wastage to effect the necessary reductions in the workforce. This will include freezing external recruitment during the period concerned, with the exception that the company reserves the right to recruit replacements for individual employees who leave and whose expertise cannot be provided by the transfer of other employees.

☐ *the extent to which wastage diminishes over time*. Turnover is almost always highest among short-service employees. Turnover studies from various organisations have given figures of 20 per cent to 40 per cent of leavers having less than three months' service. If natural wastage is used over a lengthy period, this fallout of recently recruited employees gradually ceases and turnover rates become lower among staff as their length of service increases.

❑ *the effect of impending redundancy on resignations.* The fact that the organisation is taking action to secure workforce reductions, even though this action is intended to prevent redundancies, may itself have two opposite effects on wastage:

  – Some employees (generally those with the most marketable skills and experience) may decide to leave as quickly as possible rather than run the risk of eventual redundancy. Although this may assist in achieving the staffing reductions, it may also result in the loss of a disproportionate number of the most competent staff. There is a strong case, therefore, for reassuring key staff that their services will continue to be required beyond the period of workforce reductions.

  – In other cases, staff who have been considering resignation or early retirement may postpone such decisions in the hope that they may eventually be made redundant and will then obtain the compensation they would miss if they jumped the gun. At the time of writing (summer 1999) the UK government is planning to issue a code of practice on ageism which is intended to provide a benchmark for employers' behaviour in this area. The European Court of Justice (ECJ) ruling on the Simpson case is also awaited, concerning redundancy payments to employees over the age of 65.

Despite these possible drawbacks, natural wastage remains a painless way of achieving workforce reductions. It is also widely accepted as such by employees, the trade unions and indeed society at large. For employers, the two key points are: first, to assess its likely scale as accurately as possible; second, to be aware of its down-side and leave scope for other methods.

Stopping or reducing overtime

Whether or not restrictions on the use of overtime can be used to prevent redundancy is influenced by the organisation's general overtime practices. If overtime is worked only on an occasional basis to deal with short-term peaks in demand or to cover sickness or holiday absence, it is improbable that a ban would have any significant effect on impending redundancies.

But in some organisations, overtime has become routine, most employees working regularly for several hours a week beyond their contractual weekly hours. Overtime may be so normal a feature of work in these cases that employees come to consider its availability (and payments) as a right. This does not make implementing a cessation or reduction easy – it may well be strongly opposed by employees, who will understandably react against what amounts to a cut in their normal earnings. Nevertheless, if the organisation has to reduce the workforce, this type of overtime provides a choice – maintain the practice and make employees redundant, or stop the use of routine overtime and avoid or minimise the redundancies.

The two objections often raised by managements to overtime bans are the difficulty of imposing a cut in earnings and an argument that the overtime element of the work needs to be done outside basic daily hours. There are at least two possible responses:

☐ If the impending redundancy situation is explained to, and discussed with, the employees concerned (and, if relevant, with their trade union representatives) it may well be that they will agree to priority being given to saving jobs rather than protecting earnings. It cannot be expected that this will meet with undiluted enthusiasm, but to give those concerned a say in deciding which is the lesser of two evils is surely a sensible way to proceed.

☐ Managers should be reminded that the proportion of work being done on overtime is costing considerably more (probably between some 30 and 50 per cent more) than work done within basic non-overtime hours. If the argument is that overtime is necessary because the work involved has to be done outside normal hours, a more cost-effective alternative is to recruit part-time staff on plain-time rates. By itself, this will not achieve the targeted workforce reduction but, combined with other measures (such as the use of natural wastage), it might contribute both to an avoidance of at least some redundancies and to the introduction of a more flexible way of resourcing the organisation to meet future fluctuations in demand.

Terminating the employment of non-permanent workers

The term 'permanent' is used here simply to distinguish between employees on open-ended contracts in which the only provision for termination is by notice (with no indication of when this might be), and those on other forms of contract in which a termination date earlier than normal retirement is either specified or implied. Whether the organisation makes extensive use of these forms of human resourcing is a matter of long-term strategy, as discussed in Chapter 2; but even if the core/periphery concept has not been adopted, most organisations make some use of temporary staff, casual workers or staff supplied from agencies, and are likely to have some employees on fixed-term contracts. One possible means of avoiding redundancies among permanent employees is therefore to terminate the employment of staff on these other types of contract.

Whether such terminations are either practicable or desirable depends on several factors. If the diminished requirements of the business occur within areas of work being done by one or other of these non-permanent categories, the termination of the relevant contracts is clearly indicated. The position is not so clear if the surplus of employees is expected to occur among permanent staff doing different work. The question then is whether by terminating temporary or contract staff, alternative jobs might be made available for displaced permanent staff.

If it appears that terminations among non-permanent staff would ease the redundancy situation, several issues need to be clarified before any action is taken:

☐ Are the persons concerned employees?

☐ If not, what conditions apply to the termination of the relevant contracts for services?

☐ If they are employees, might their termination give rise to redundancy rights?

Employees or not?

Non-employees

There are two types of 'employment' in which the persons concerned are not employees in the formal or legal sense:

□ *staff supplied by agencies*, such as office 'temps' or contract drawing-office staff. They may be either employees of the organisation which supplies them or, more probably, self-employed. Their services are provided through commercial contracts between the agency and the user or client, not through contracts of employment between them as individuals and the client organisation. The termination of such contracts by the client does not, therefore, constitute dismissal or redundancy.

□ *self-employed individuals*, such as freelance software writers, who provide their services directly to the client organisation – but under contracts for services, not contracts of employment. The termination of such contracts does not constitute redundancy unless there is a successful challenge by the individual to their own self-employed status. This would be highly unlikely if a written contract for services existed, but might be an issue if the working arrangements had been entered into too casually, and without clear definition and agreement. The definition of self-employed status has been a source of legal difficulty for many years, and is complicated by Inland Revenue interpretations. Important features of self-employment include:

  – the existence of a genuine commercial relationship
  – the freedom (and practice) of the self-employed person to work for other clients
  – the absence of any obligation by the client to provide work, and the freedom of the self-employed person to accept or reject offers of work
  – a low level of control by the client over how the self-employed person works
  – often, the provision by the self-employed person of their own materials, equipment and premises
  – no holiday and sickness pay.

The absence of Pay As You Earn (PAYE) and National Insurance (NI) deductions is not conclusive evidence of self-employment, because the courts (and/or the Inland Revenue) might still decide the reality of the working arrangement was one of employment – in which case back-payments of tax and NI become due as well as the possibility of redundancy compensation.

Employees

Non-permanent staff who are employees include:

☐ *temporary employees*. In any general sense, the law does not recognise temporary employees as a distinct category. An employee is an employee – whether or not the employment contract is open-ended and regardless of a 'temporary' label. The main issue that influences employment rights (including redundancy rights) is the length of continuous service, as explained later in this chapter. The dismissal of temporary staff because the employer has no (or less) need for employees engaged on their particular kind of work is potentially as much a case of redundancy as the similar dismissal of permanent staff. Whether or not either qualify for statutory redundancy depends on the same length-of-service criteria. There is one exception to this – the termination of employment when it has been a term of the contract that employment will cease on completion of a specified task or set of circumstances, though not on a specified date. (If the date is stated, this is a fixed-term contract for which different provisions apply; see below.) Known as a contract for performance, the cessation of employment when the specified work ends is not classed as a dismissal and therefore redundancy does not occur – although the courts require clear proof that such a contractual provision exists. It is important to note, however, that in many redundancy situations the termination of employees on performance contracts has to be considered before the normal completion of these contracts. Such premature termination of a performance contract does constitute dismissal – and therefore gives rise to possible redundancy entitlements if the length-of-service criteria are met.

☐ *seasonal workers*. There are a number of occupations in which employment is seasonal – for example, in the catering and agricultural industries. Generally speaking, seasonal workers are employed either on performance contracts (eg 'until the end of the hop-picking season', date unspecified) or on fixed-term contracts (eg 'until the hotel closes on 31 October'). In the former case, the question of redundancy does not arise if employment ceases at the end of the season. In the latter case, the position is the same as for any other employee working on a fixed-term contract – see below. Seasonal workers can qualify for statutory redundancy payments if they build up sufficient continuity of service (see the later section in this chapter dealing with the two years' service criterion).

- *employees on fixed-term contracts*. A fixed-term contract is one that specifies its expiry date. Staff on fixed-term contracts are, of course, employees and have full statutory employment rights in most circumstances. Subject to certain exceptions, the non-renewal of a fixed-term contract also constitutes dismissal – so a normal redundancy situation can occur if such a contract is not renewed because of a cessation or diminution of the employer's requirement for employees in that particular kind of work. The two exceptions are:
  - when, in a contract for two years or more, an agreed clause has been included in which the employee waives the right to redundancy compensation on non-renewal
  - when the non-renewal is by mutual consent – that is, the employee as well as the employer does not want the contract renewed.

  It must be remembered, however, that the premature termination of a fixed-term contract (even if it has a waiver clause about non-renewal) does constitute dismissal. Whether redundancy rights accrue in this instance, or in non-renewals not covered by a waiver clause, depends on whether the length of service meets the statutory service criteria (see later section) – and, of course, the existence of a genuine redundancy situation as the reason for the dismissal.

- *casual workers*. There has been much confusion in the past about the employment status of casual workers – people to whom an organisation may offer work as and when it is available, but who may not be under any formal, contractual obligation to accept work when it is offered. Many such workers are used in the catering industry. The hotel or restaurant has a list of casuals whom it contacts from time to time owing to the pressure of work or staff absences. There is no contractual requirement for the worker to come into work when contacted: he or she is free (at least in theory) to say they are busy elsewhere or are just not interested this time. Employers have often assumed that workers of this kind are not employees within the meaning of relevant employment legislation, and that to terminate their employment does not, therefore, constitute redundancy – even though the length of their working relationship with the organisation may have exceeded the two-year minimum period for entitlement to redundancy compensation.

At one time, the courts tended to the view that the absence of any contractual obligation to work when asked or invited to do so indicated a status other than that of normal employment and, in such cases, claims for redundancy compensation failed. More recently, the opposite view has prevailed and casuals are treated as employees, not least because in practice the apparent freedom of the casual worker to choose when or when not to work is very restricted and sometimes illusory. The following case illustrates this:

> A large London hotel claimed that a dismissed casual worker was not an employee because he was not obliged to accept work when offered. But evidence was given that should the worker concerned have ever refused the casual work he was offered, he would not have been offered any more work. This was decided by the Employment Appeal Tribunal (EAT) to equate to the requirements of a contract of employment so, again, he was held to be an employee. (*Four Seasons* v *Hamarat*)

Of course, casual workers can only qualify for redundancy payments if they have been employed for sufficient time to meet the two-year service criterion, which is explained in a later section of this chapter. Here, it is sufficient to note that a typical 'on/off' working pattern for a casual worker will not necessarily break continuity of employment if the 'off' periods are of short duration. Although their employment status at law may still be open to question in some circumstances, for all practical purposes, casual workers are best considered as normal employees and it should not, therefore, be assumed that redundancy liabilities can be avoided by the use of casual labour.

Termination conditions for non-employees

Once it has been established that a particular person is not an employee, it is necessary to consider how the arrangement can be brought to an end without incurring legal or contractual penalties. The termination of contracts for services needs care.

These contracts may include termination provisions, such as the giving of notice, or have penalty clauses for premature termination if the contract has a specified duration. Such clauses are not an argument for not proceeding with termination, but any costs involved (or adverse effects on important business relationships) may have to be balanced against the benefits of the terminations in enabling the organisation to avoid making its own employees redundant.

The two-year service criterion for non-permanent staff

All dismissals of employees, whether on permanent, temporary, or fixed-term contracts, are subject to the same length-of-service criterion to qualify for statutory redundancy rights. The employee must have served a period of at least two years' continuous service, although at the time of writing, (summer 1999) there were proposals to reduce this period. Two preliminary issues may be noted:

□ From a non-legal viewpoint, dismissing someone (permanent or temporary) with less than two years' service because his or her services are no longer required will probably be seen by the person concerned and their colleagues as redundancy. The fact that no statutory rights and obligations arise will not alter the reality of dismissal – indeed, the absence of any redundancy compensation if the employer does not add to what is due by statute may well make the dismissal appear harsher than when 'real' redundancy occurs. Organisations need to consider very carefully the impact of such dismissals on employee morale and on their general reputation before assuming that one way of avoiding the adverse effects of redundancy is to dismiss short-service employees.

□ The statutory redundancy rights that an employee acquires after completing two years' continuous service are wider than simply entitlement to specified payments. They include consultation rights, a right to be fairly selected for redundancy, and an obligation by the employer to consider the offer of alternative work. Chapter 5 goes into these matters in detail.

The requirement to have at least two years' continuous service to qualify for redundancy rights may seem clear-cut. This is the case for any employee who has had no break in working time or attendance. But with temporary and seasonal staff, and for employees on a succession of fixed-term contracts, there can be circumstances in which the application of the two-year rule is much more complicated. This arises because the statute provides for certain kinds of absence, working less than the minimum number of hours, breaks in working, and even periods of non-employment, to be disregarded in calculating continuous service. (The provisions that apply to breaks during the period of a normal contract of employment, eg lengthy sickness absences, are dealt with in Chapter 9, for the contract normally continues during such breaks.) Here, the provisions applying to breaks during which there is no contract in existence are examined:

☐ *Temporary and seasonal employees*. Temporary employees are sometimes employed to work for quite regular periods, each working spell followed by a break. An example might be a school cleaner who works only during each school term. A seasonal worker, too, might regularly work in a hotel from March to November each year, with a break of three winter months when the hotel is closed. Do working arrangements of these kinds form continuous employment? The legislation says that periods when there is no contract of employment may count towards continuous service when

    – the break is caused by 'a temporary cessation of work' (not defined in the Act)

    – by 'arrangement or custom', the person concerned is 'regarded as continuing in the employment of his employer for any or all purposes' – again, a phrase not defined further.

It is impossible to give a precise interpretation of these two very generalised clauses. The principles can best be illustrated by an example of how the courts have interpreted them:

    A tanker driver delivered fuel oil only during the winter months, working approximately six months on and six months off. Each period of work was treated as a new, temporary employment contract, but when the employers decided not to offer him any more winter work, he claimed he had built up over two years' continuous service. The Court of Appeal (CA) decided against him. They considered the length of the non-working periods was too long relative to the periods of work, saying that to qualify for continuous service, the breaks should be 'relatively short'.

More complicated situations can occur when the pattern of work has been irregular. In cases where the periods of work and the breaks between them have varied in duration, the CA has said that the whole history of the employment should be considered in the round, not just the narrow issue of the duration of any one break of service.

From the many cases about the interpretation of 'temporary cessation' when there have been breaks in employment, it is evident that the factors to consider are:

– the length of the break or breaks, relative to the length of periods of employment: the greater the break on this relative basis, the less likely it is that continuity has been established

– whether or not the breaks and re-engagements form a regular pattern: the greater the regularity, the more likely it is that employment will be treated as continuous

– what the employer and employee intended

– whether anything is done during the break which maintains some type of relationship between the employer and the employee – such as asking the employee to keep in regular contact or be ready, if asked, to come in for relief or other work

– particularly where an irregular pattern of working spells is involved, whether the only reason for the breaks is that for a temporary period, no work is available. In other words, it is reasonable to assume that had there been no cessation of the work, employment would have continued.

All these points should certainly be examined before it is assumed that the dismissal of a temporary worker will not be a statutory redundancy. The issue is of particular importance for employees of this type whose working relationship with the organisation apart from short or regular breaks may have extended over many years.

☐ *Employees on fixed-term contracts*. As noted earlier, the expiry and non-renewal of a fixed-term contract constitutes dismissal, thus giving the employee eligibility to pursue claims for unfair dismissal and/or redundancy provided the standard two-year service criterion is met. However, these statutory rights can be set aside if the written contract (or a later written agreement made during the currency of the contract) includes a waiver clause. The use of waiver clauses whereby the employee agrees that unfair dismissal or redundancy claims will not be pursued in the event of non-renewal are a common practice, although at the time of writing there were proposals to outlaw them in relation to unfair dismissal. An example of a redundancy clause follows:

> The expiry and non-renewal of this contract for whatever reasons shall not constitute grounds for an action for redundancy, and the employee agrees not to pursue such action at that time.

Note, however, that waivers of redundancy rights cannot be included in fixed-term contracts of less than two years' duration – and this creates the possibility of such rights accruing if contracts for shorter periods are renewed and total service thereby accumulates to or more than two years' duration.

In the absence of waiver clauses, two factors require examination when deciding whether the termination of a fixed-term contract involves two years' continuous service and a potential entitlement to redundancy compensation:

- Has total service accumulated beyond two years by one or more renewals of the contract, without intervening breaks? If so, this total service counts – not just the length of the current contract.
- If there have been breaks between renewals, should they be discounted on the same grounds as explained above for breaks in temporary or seasonal employment? The law applies the same criteria.

A leading case about breaks between fixed-term contracts illustrates how very sizeable redundancy entitlements can be accrued, despite each contract being for less than 12 months and short breaks occurring between each contract:

> A teacher employed by a county council was engaged at the beginning of each academic year in September on a fixed-term contract which expired at the end of each summer term. After eight years, there came a year when she was not re-engaged and the question as to whether she had one term's or eight

years' continuity of employment became a matter of dispute. The case went all the way to the House of Lords. Their Lordships decided that the statutory provision for continuity to count if the breaks in employment have been caused by temporary non-availability of work applied just as much to breaks between fixed-term contracts as it did to similar breaks between temporary or seasonal employment contracts. Each of the teacher's breaks had occurred because, in the words of the statute, there had been 'a temporary cessation of work' – so all her service counted as continuous. (*Ford* v *Warwickshire County Council*)

This case illustrates the care that needs to be taken in examining the precise nature of each individual's employment contract and history before deciding that a dismissal will contribute to a redundancy avoidance plan.

One general point emerges from this study of the complexities of different forms of employment and different ways in which employees can acquire two years or more of continuous employment. This is that when redundancy is imminent, the priority in terminating various forms of contract is best placed on those which are not contracts of employment. In other words, the use of non-employees should be stopped first, and only when this has been done should consideration be given to the termination of those temporary employees who do not appear to have the two years of continuous service needed to qualify for statutory redundancy rights.

Retraining and redeployment

There is a legal as well as moral obligation to take all reasonable steps to identify and offer suitable alternative employment to an employee who would otherwise be dismissed on redundancy grounds. The redeployment obligation is not a statutory requirement: it has emerged from case-law – in particular from a ruling by the CA – that employers should do what they can, so far as this is reasonable, to find alternative work. It is also important to note that an employee cannot be said to have been fairly dismissed for redundancy unless there is no work available that he or she could have been required to do within the terms of the contract of employment. Therefore the search for possible redeployment opportunities needs to be widely conducted.

In terms of good practice it is also necessary to consider work that differs from the employee's contractual duties but for which the displaced employee might, with their agreement, be trained. There is no specific legal requirement, either statutory or in case-law, to provide retraining to help employees take up alternative work, but in practice there are often circumstances in which this can make a major contribution to the avoidance of redundancy and contribute towards the development of a multi-skilled workforce.

One form of redeployment may be made possible by the action discussed in the previous section – the termination of contracts for the supply of agency staff and the like. It may be that there is little or no diminution in the work they are engaged on, but that by terminating their use, jobs can be found for permanent staff displaced from other work. Similarly, a freeze on external recruitment may well result in vacancies that can be filled by the transfer of otherwise redundant employees. Redeployment may also be possible to new jobs which the organisation is creating in parts of the business unaffected by the factors that have led to impending redundancy elsewhere.

In large organisations, these various types of redeployment opportunity can be difficult to identify and utilise unless there is co-ordinated action across the whole business, and co-operation between the managements of various parts of the business. Too often, the manager of one unit or division will refuse to consider the transfer of a potentially redundant employee from elsewhere in the organisation and insist on external recruitment or an appointment made from within his or her own staff. This not only represents a poor standard of management practice but may also open the organisation to claims for compensation for unfair redundancy dismissal. So far as the law and the courts are concerned, the onus of providing alternative employment falls on the employer – the organisation as a corporate body – and not on any narrower managerial concept of internally separate sections or divisions.

The risk of dealing too narrowly with redeployment has increased in recent years with the trend towards devolved or decentralised management systems and organisational structures. Authority to recruit and dismiss employees has in many cases been devolved to the managers of cost centres or internal business units, in line with many of the principles of the flexible organisation. It is rightly argued that central control over all aspects of recruitment and dismissal prevents unit or sectional managers from managing and motivating their own workforces effectively, and introduces unnecessary delay in important decisions about each unit's resourcing. How can this principle of devolved management be reconciled with the legal requirement (and the expectation of employees and trade unions) for organisations to act corporately in managing potential redundancies? A public-sector example illustrates these issues:

> A large local authority adopted an organisational policy of maximising managerial devolution and established a large number of internal business units, each with its own budget and full control of its own staffing. Managers of business units had authority to decide their own staffing levels and to make their own recruitment and dismissal decisions without reference to the small, strategic, central personnel function. There was concern, however, that in a redundancy situation, a dismissal within one unit might coincide with a suitable alternative job being vacant in another. One of the very few centrally imposed personnel procedures was consequently a requirement that business units must inform the central personnel function of any impending redundancies and not effect such dismissals until the central function had checked the availability of alternative work across the whole organisation. Units were also required to give priority consideration to displaced employees before moving to external recruitment.

A general training policy aimed at broadening all employees' range of skills can, as Chapter 2 argued, be part of the organisation's long-term measures to avoid redundancy. But retraining can also make a more immediate contribution in a real redundancy situation, and may be used either for a whole group of employees or for individuals. The practicability of retraining as an immediate redundancy avoidance measure is dependent on several factors:

☐ the suitability of the displaced employees for retraining – and their acceptance of this alternative to redundancy

☐ the timescale of the training needed to bring an inexperienced employee up to an acceptable standard

- training costs – relative to the alternative costs of redundancy
- whether previous pay, earnings levels or other conditions of service need to be protected during the training period
- managerial attitudes – are supervisors and managers willing to co-operate in retraining and, particularly where individual employees are concerned, give the necessary attention to on-the-job coaching and encouragement?

One of the main obstacles to overcome is too restricted a view being taken about the suitability of displaced employees for retraining. For example, if the organisation's conventional training programmes are centred on young recruits, managers may assume that employees in their 40s or 50s will be slower to train or even be unadaptable to new work. This stereotype of the dog being too old to learn new tricks may also sap the confidence of the displaced employees themselves. Both they and the managers concerned may be difficult to convince that in very many cases people can be shown to be far more adaptable than had been initially assumed.

Retraining has become progressively practicable in recent years as training methods have become more flexible. In addition to the two conventional methods of the full-time course and 'sitting by Nellie', there are now self-learning systems, computer-based training programmes, a wide variety of part-time and distance learning packages, and a considerable emphasis on the value of coaching and mentoring. The particular methods to adopt depend on the specific circumstances of each case. In general, however, course-based programmes may best contribute to the retraining of groups of employees, and job-based programmes supported by self-learning and mentoring best suit individual employees.

There are three main sets of arguments for the use of retraining – costs, employee morale, and the organisation's reputation:

- Efficient organisations should know the per capita cost of training for a particular job and be able to calculate this figure for jobs being considered in a retraining context. This should include the time of trainers and supervisors, the cost of training equipment and materials, and the cost of low output before full competence is reached. To set against this, when retraining is being considered, are the cost of redundancy compensation and the cost of recruitment (either of an externally recruited trainee or of a fully trained person). It may then be shown that redundancy costs of, say, £8,000 plus recruitment costs of £4,000 are considerably more than the costs of retraining.

☐ The beneficial effects of a retraining policy apply not only to the employees who thereby escape redundancy. The whole workforce will recognise the organisation's efforts, and morale generally will benefit – an important issue, given the very adverse effect that redundancy dismissals can have on the attitudes and commitment of employees at large. It is a central theme of redundancy management that it should pay attention to the effects of redundancy on the employees who remain, as well as on those who might have to go.

☐ The organisation's general reputation as a good employer is also aided by a retraining policy. Maintaining this reputation may not seem a priority in a recessionary period, but this overlooks the need to be recognised as a good employer in better times when staff shortages, rather than surpluses, may be a major problem.

Retirement measures

Chapter 2 referred to the effect of the organisation's standard retirement and pension provisions on staff turnover. When redundancy becomes imminent, there may also be short-term retirement measures which can be used to reduce the incidence of redundancy dismissals. The three main options are:

☐ to require the retirement of employees who have reached normal retirement age but have so far been permitted to continue in employment

☐ if the pension scheme includes early retirement provisions, encouraging employees to apply to retire early. How this would operate depends very much on the rules of the particular pension scheme: all that can be suggested here is that this avenue be explored

☐ in addition to any standard early-retirement options – or if none exist, or for employees who have their own personal

pension plans – perhaps offering specific financial inducements to take retirement. These may take the form of crediting the employee with more years of pensionable service
than have actually been worked (eg the 'added years' provisions for retirements 'in the interests of the efficiency of the
service' which apply to many public-sector schemes) or could
be a lump-sum payment to purchase additional pension
benefit.

Although the encouragement of retirement may well ease the
redundancy situation or create jobs for displaced younger staff,
it needs to be handled with considerable care. Particular points
to be heeded are as follows:

□ There is a need to check the contractual and statutory position of employees who are over the normal retirement age
and who may be required to retire. Unless such a requirement is included in their contractual conditions and there is
no ambiguity about the normal retirement age, it may be
challenged as unfair dismissal, or they may be able to establish a right to redundancy compensation. Age limits are
dealt with in detail in Chapter 9, but the general principle is
that no statutory entitlement arises after the organisation's
normal retiring age, or after the 65th birthday if there is no
normal retiring age. There may be a lack of clarity, however,
as to what the organisation's normal retiring age is, particularly if this has been dealt with flexibly in the past.

□ Great care needs to be taken when encouraging or approving
early retirements to avoid any implication of discriminatory
treatment as between men and women. This applies to all
aspects of retirement including age criteria, eligibility for pensions, and any special pension enhancements offered as an
incentive to take early retirement. Note particularly that
equality of treatment applies as much to men as to women.
In a leading case decided by the ECJ, a man made redundant
at the age of 52 was not then entitled under his contracted-
out occupational pension scheme to an immediate pension,
though a woman of the same age would have been. The ECJ
decided this was contrary to Article 119 of the Treaty of
Rome – men and women must have equal access to pension
payments.

□ If retirements are being used as an alternative to redundancy, it is important that they are handled in a way that avoids any impression that employees are being put under pressure to resign. Resignation under pressure is likely, if challenged, to equate to constructive dismissal.

□ Before publicising an early-retirement scheme, thought needs to be given to how requests for retirement are to be handled from employees whom the organisation wishes to retain. It is often necessary to make clear that not all such requests can be accommodated.

□ If the intention is for retirements to be an alternative to redundancy, and for inducements such as pension enhancements to be paid instead of (not in addition to) redundancy payments, employees must resign (not be dismissed) and this position must be clearly explained when the scheme is launched. Further, the retirement process is best completed before any formal redundancy processes are started, in order to avoid confusion between retirements and redundancy terminations.

Volunteers for redundancy

Seeking volunteers for redundancy is probably the next most common or favoured method after natural wastage of avoiding compulsory redundancies. It does not, of course, avoid the payment of redundancy compensation, but it often enables an organisation to effect quite major workforce reductions without having to dismiss any employees other than those who express a willingness to go. Indeed, organisations have not infrequently underestimated the number of employees who will respond to a voluntary scheme and then had some difficulty in deciding which volunteers to accept.

Before considering the details of a scheme, there is one key point to bear in mind. This is that to meet the statutory definition of redundancy there must be a dismissal. 'Voluntary redundancy' is therefore a legal misnomer. Technically, employees must be invited to volunteer to be dismissed – not to resign. The point is of less importance for employers than it was when statutory redundancy payments were subsidised from a government fund, because at that time the subsidy was withheld unless there had been a dismissal. However, it still has importance in the public sector where the legitimacy of redundancy payments may be challenged by the Audit Commission. Adherence to the principle also helps to protect all employers from claims for redundancy payments by employees who resign – either when jumping the gun on eventual redundancy dismissals or when taking early retirement. An early tribunal case illustrates this:

> An employer launched a voluntary redundancy scheme and a woman employee submitted her name as a volunteer. However, she was only two years away from her normal retirement date, so her application to join the scheme was turned down. She then resigned on an early retirement basis and claimed redundancy compensation on the grounds that there was a redundancy situation. The court turned down her claim, saying the employers were entitled to decide not to effect a redundancy dismissal, and that her decision to retire was a voluntary resignation. (*Messent* v *Bowater Ripper*)

There are four main factors to consider in designing a voluntary scheme:

☐ How many volunteers in which kinds of work is the scheme planned to secure?

☐ What inducements are to be offered (if any) in addition to statutory entitlements?

☐ How widely is the net to be cast – which employees will be invited to volunteer?

☐ How are volunteers to be selected if more apply than are needed; and how are those volunteers to be handled whom the organisation does not wish to release?

There is obviously no point in seeking volunteers from work sectors in which there is no projected surplus of employees, or where vacancies could not be used for redeployment. Yet some organisations still mount schemes that invite interest across the whole organisation – only to be faced with far more volunteers than can be accepted, and consequently having to disappoint people who wish to depart. The reason sometimes given for this practice is that to offer terms to some employees and not others causes dissatisfaction, or that the scheme is being used to provide information about employee attitudes across the whole organisation which may be of future use. In general, it is very doubtful if these reasons outweigh the disadvantages of raising expectations which cannot be met. In most cases, volunteers are best sought only from persons in jobs that are in surplus or that could provide alternative work for employees displaced from other work sectors.

Statutory entitlements are of course mandatory. The question in many schemes is the extent to which the organisation will enhance or go beyond these payments as an inducement to volunteers. Many organisations have adopted a better scale of payments and included this within their redundancy agreements with the trade unions. Non-unionised organisations may also include an enhanced scale of payments within their standard schedule of employee benefits. Either way, it is helpful to decide on the scale of payments as a general policy issue rather than make *ad hoc* decisions whenever a redundancy situation occurs. It is a matter of judgment (balanced, perhaps, by information about the general practice among similar organisations) as to how far it is necessary or desirable to go beyond the statutory sums, and in practice, the range of payments varies widely between different organisations and economic sectors. It may also be necessary to take the organisation's financial situation into account. Payment levels that may have seemed acceptable if a scale was agreed in boom times could be financially damaging when large-scale redundancy becomes necessary as a way of cutting costs in a company with an adverse cash flow.

In determining and announcing the organisation's own scale, a distinction needs to be made between payments to which employees acquire a contractual right, and those the organisation makes on an *ex gratia* basis. Contractual payments may accrue in two ways:

□ by inclusion in collective agreements that are, explicitly or implicitly, incorporated into individual contracts of employment

□ by inclusion in schedules of terms and conditions of employment that are issued to all employees – unless these state clearly that the redundancy payments may be made only at the employer's discretion.

The announcement of voluntary schemes needs to specify whether all volunteers, or only some, will be accepted – and indicate the basis of any selection. Ambiguity about such selection leads to allegations of unfairness which, although not necessarily open to legal challenge, may nevertheless damage employee morale and staff–management relations. The underlying problem is often that with a surplus of volunteers, the understandable tendency is to choose the less satisfactory. This leads to the complaint from hard-working, highly competent staff that it is the less satisfactory employees who benefit from attractive redundancy terms, whereas effective staff have to work through to normal retirement. Ideally, therefore, voluntary schemes are used when it is evident that all volunteers can be accepted and no selection is necessary. When this is not possible, schemes should try to avoid being so attractive that they generate far more volunteers than are needed; in any event, it should be made very clear in advance that the organisation may have to be selective.

Volunteers who cannot be released should have the reasons explained, be given the opportunity of explaining why they volunteered, and perhaps be counselled about either further career progression or later opportunities for early retirement. If they are told they are indispensable, this should be reflected in their appraisal ratings and performance payments.

To avoid problems so far as possible, it is good practice to handle a voluntary scheme by a two-stage process:

☐ In the first instance, employees are invited to indicate, without commitment, a possible interest in volunteering – the outcome to be subject on the employer's side to a willingness to release and, on the employee's side, to satisfactory terms.

☐ Each of these provisional applications can then be discussed individually and taken further only if all aspects are satisfactory to both parties.

Key points

☐ There are many measures that can be taken to avoid compulsory redundancies when it becomes evident that employee surpluses are probable.

- These measures include:
  - natural wastage
  - restrictions on recruitment
  - restrictions on overtime
  - terminating the use of non-permanent employees and agency staff
  - retirement measures
  - seeking volunteers.
- Natural wastage is the least painful or costly measure, though its prolonged use may result in distortions in the constitution of the workforce.
- The freezing or limitation of recruitment can be used to support natural wastage and create vacancies to which potentially redundant employees can be redeployed.
- Stopping or reducing overtime may reduce costs as well as saving jobs, though in practice its use is probably limited to the cessation of routine overtime working, not to overtime needed to cope with temporary work peaks.
- In considering the termination of non-permanent employees, it is important to distinguish between those who are employees and others who are not – such as self-employed and agency/contract workers. The priority for termination is best placed on the non-employees.
- Before terminating contracts for services (or contracts for the supply of workers) it is advisable to check whether the contracts include penalty clauses for early termination.
- In considering the termination of non-permanent employees (such as temporary, seasonal or fixed-term contract staff) it is necessary to identify those who may have acquired redundancy rights through their length of continuous service (two years or more).
- In assessing continuous service, it must be noted that some short or regular breaks of service caused by the non-availability of work may have to be discounted.
- The termination of a performance contract on completion of the task or work for which it was agreed does not constitute dismissal and no redundancy rights then accrue.
- There is a legal obligation (under case-law) to take reasonable

steps to find alternative work for a potentially redundant employee.

☐ There is no such obligation to provide retraining, but the use of retraining can be a major contribution to the avoidance of enforced redundancies and can contribute to a multi-skilled workforce.

☐ Managers may initially take too narrow a view of the practicality of retraining: employees are often more adaptable and trainable than conventional employment practices indicate.

☐ A retraining policy may be less costly than paying redundancy compensation and incurring the costs of recruiting fully experienced staff.

☐ Retraining also helps maintain employee morale within the whole workforce and benefits the organisation's external reputation as a good employer.

☐ Some workforce reductions (or vacancies suitable for re-deployed staff) may be achieved by requiring the retirement of employees above normal retiring age and/or by encouraging early retirements.

☐ Care needs to be taken in enforcing retirement if there is uncertainty about the organisation's normal retirement age. Also, men and women should be treated equally.

☐ Some additional benefits (eg added pension benefits) may need to be offered to induce early retirements.

☐ There must be no implication of coercion, otherwise a retirement resignation may be interpreted as constructive dismissal.

☐ Seeking volunteers to be made redundant is probably the most extensively used measure after natural wastage.

☐ Volunteers should be asked to indicate their willingness to be dismissed on grounds of redundancy – not asked to resign.

☐ In launching a voluntary scheme, it should be made clear whether all volunteers will be accepted, or whether the organisation may have to be selective.

☐ Inducements to volunteer generally involve payments above the statutory limit – the amount is a matter of judgment and comparison with other similar organisations. Too high a level may generate an embarrassingly large number of volunteers: too low a level may prove ineffective.

☐ Employees who volunteer but cannot be accepted need explanation and counselling.

☐ A two-stage process to a voluntary scheme is recommended: an invitation to express a provisional no-commitment interest in leaving followed by individual discussions and final decisions.

4 WHAT IS REDUNDANCY?

The effective management of redundancy involves an understanding of the impact on those concerned of their loss of employment, the fear and uncertainty it may create among the employees who survive, the stress it may cause for managers who have the unpleasant task of deciding who should go, and the legal requirements to which the various decisions and procedures must conform. Action that, although well-intentioned, overlooks some aspect of the law can lead to an expensive legal settlement. The starting-point for understanding the legal context is to be clear, from the viewpoint of tribunals and the courts, about just what constitutes redundancy. This may seem obvious but, as this chapter explains, there have been many cases where organisations or employees have misunderstood the legal definition.

'Redundancy', as used in general conversation, can mean different things to different people. Employees who have just been dismissed and told their services are no longer needed may feel the word indicates consignment to the scrap-heap. Others sometimes consider the term a smoke-screen, used by managements as a generalised explanation for dismissals that have really been effected for other reasons – a view given some substance by a survey in 1992 in which over 200 organisations (46 per cent of the total surveyed) admitted that some dismissals for incompetence had been described as redundancies.

Some managers and employee representatives, taking too narrow a view, assume redundancy can occur only when a workforce is being reduced in size or only when an organisation's workload is shrinking. Others, including some personnel managers, sometimes talk of voluntary redundancy, as though resignations as well as dismissals can be classified in statutory terms as redundancies. Outplacement consultants or other redundancy counsellors, conscious of the damaging psychological impact of any implication that an employee has been 'scrapped', have argued that it is jobs that become redundant, not people.

At a detailed legal level, there have been many misunderstandings by managers and employees about such matters as the rights to statutory redundancy payments of staff on fixed-term or temporary contracts, the definition of 'a week's pay' as used in calculating redundancy payments, or the employment position of staff in a business that has been transferred from one owner to another. A common misconception among employees is that there is a right to have selection for redundancy decided on the basis of 'last in, first out' (often referred to as LIFO).

Redundancy is an emotional subject – both for those who lose their jobs and for managers who have the unpleasant task of relaying the bad news. What is often overlooked is the effect redundancies can have on employees who are not directly affected but whose sense of job security is undermined by the fear that they may be the next to go. If redundancies are handled insensitively, this will also damage the organisation's internal and external reputation. That many managers are reluctant to deal with redundancy clearly and positively is indicated by the many euphemisms used to avoid the hard truths about people losing their jobs. Three examples from company announcements about impending workforce reductions illustrate this:

> We have decided with reluctance that we will have to let a number of our employees go.

> We regret that some of our people will be disadvantaged in employment terms by a downsizing programme.

> The de-layering of our company structure will unfortunately require enforced external career moves for some staff.

At the other end of the spectrum from this type of obfuscation is the harsh practice in some organisations of informing employees summarily of their redundancy on a Friday afternoon, requiring them to clear their desks or lockers immediately and then leave the premises. Both the soft and hard approaches can lead to difficulties for the employer, the former sometimes giving rise to complaints about imprecise information in the consultative phase, the latter engendering a resentful reaction and the suspicion that personal antagonism has been involved – and so causing complaints to be made to an employment tribunal about unfair selection and dismissal procedures, as well as about a total lack of consultation.

The legal definition

It is highly desirable and good management practice to handle all redundancies sensitively and in ways that help those affected retain their self-respect and self-confidence. But the effective management of redundancies requires more than sympathy and assistance for those who lose their jobs. It must be done in accordance with the law, because the employer's position is seriously damaged if individual employees or trade unions are able to establish legal flaws in the process – however well-intentioned this process may have been. Moreover, falling foul of the legislation can be expensive, costs occurring at the very time that an organisation is often experiencing financial difficulty. Redundancy legislation and its associated case-law is one of the most complex areas of employment law, and a starting-point for a sound approach to the detailed aspects of redundancy management must be a clear understanding of the legal definitions.

The statutory definition of redundancy is given in the Employment Rights Act 1996 (ERA). The first and basic criterion for an employee to be considered redundant is that he or she must have been dismissed. This dismissal must then be mainly or wholly attributable to one of the following situations:

☐ The employer has ceased (or intends to cease) carrying on the business in which the employee was employed; or ceases (or intends to cease) carrying out this business at the place where the employee was employed.

☐ The requirements for employees to carry out work 'of a particular kind' have ceased or diminished (or are expected to cease or diminish), either in the business as a whole or in the place where the person was employed.

Each of these criteria needs further explanation.

Dismissal

The requirement for there to have been a dismissal before an employee becomes entitled to statutory redundancy rights is of fundamental importance, and has been the subject of much misunderstanding, particularly by employees who resign when redundancy seems imminent but before formal redundancy dismissal notices have been issued. 'Jumping the gun' in this way invalidates claims for statutory redundancy payments, as the following example shows:

> In October one year, a computer company told all the employees at one of its sites that the factory would close at the end of the following September, and that they would then all receive severance payments. One employee found another job, left, and claimed a redundancy payment. The EAT rejected his claim, stating that the employer's announcement of the factory closure was not a dismissal. The date of closure had been stated clearly, but there had been no indication of precisely when employment as an individual would have come to an end. (*ICL* v *Kennedy*)

Occasionally, employers make mistakes about the redundancy implications of resignations. For example:

> An employee had informed her employers that she was applying to become an adopter and would have to leave at short notice as soon as a child became available for adoption – although she did not know when this would be. After she had told her employers this, but before a child became available, her job came to an end and she was declared redundant. The employers claimed that no redundancy payment was due because she had already announced her resignation, but an industrial tribunal disagreed. They pointed out that a statement of intention to resign at some future date did not constitute a resignation. She had been dismissed on grounds of redundancy and was therefore entitled to the appropriate statutory payment. (*Mabert* v *Ellerman Lines*)

The distinction between resignation and dismissal, and the circumstances that equate to dismissal, are not quite as clear-cut as may initially appear. So legislation provides definitions not just of redundancy but of dismissal itself. These state that in addition to the straightforward termination of a contract of employment by an employer (with or without notice), a redundancy dismissal may occur in the following circumstances:

- when there has been a failure to permit a woman to return to work after statutory maternity absence
- when a fixed-term contract expires and is not renewed on the same terms
- when an employee resigns after being given notice but before the notice period expires
- when an employee leaves and claims constructive dismissal – that is, the employer has behaved in such a way as to amount to a fundamental breach of the employment contract, so justifying the employee leaving without giving notice.

Whether statutory redundancy occurs in any of these circumstances depends on the facts of each case. In the event of an employee claiming a redundancy payment (and the employer resisting this) it would be for the employer to provide evidence to an employment tribunal that there were other reasons for the employee's implied dismissal than those defined by the statutory redundancy criteria – such as conduct or capability. The onus would not be on the employee to prove redundancy because the statute includes a presumption that redundancy has occurred, unless the employer can show a different reason. Note, however, that if the employer claims that no dismissal took place (ie that the employee resigned), the onus is on the employee to prove that dismissal occurred (though not necessarily the reasons).

The two key points are:

- the need for a dismissal to occur (directly or by implication) before a statutory redundancy occurs
- the onus on the employer to prove the reason for a dismissal if the employee's claim that a redundancy has occurred is disputed.

The whole or main reason

For a dismissal to comply with the statutory definition, redundancy as defined must be the main or whole reason. There may be dismissals in which other reasons than a change in the needs of the business are involved, but these must be subsidiary (ie in a relatively minor form) to the redundancy factors if redundancy is to be established. As a general rule, dismissal in such cases should not have occurred if only the non-redundancy reasons applied.

In any disputed case, whether based mainly or wholly on redundancy, an employment tribunal must consider only whether or not the redundancy reasons were genuine – not whether the redundancy decision itself was sound in business terms. The employer must, of course, show that a redundancy dismissal was based on what the EAT once described as reasonable information, reasonably acquired, and was not capricious. But it is not for a tribunal to substitute its own assessment of the requirements of the business for that of the employer.

Actual, intended or expected changes

There are three conditions in which redundancy dismissals can be effected within the statutory criteria:

- when a business (in whole or in part) has actually ceased
- when there is an intention to close all or part of a business – that is, when an employer has taken such a decision but before it has been fully effected
- when there is an expectation that the requirements of the business for a particular type of employee will cease or diminish.

So it can be legitimate to make employees redundant based on plans and forecasts – not only when work has actually come to an end.

Redundancies based on expectations or forecasts may be challenged by employees or their trade unions on the grounds that the assumptions are inadequate or inaccurate. The test in any such case is one of reasonableness and the question a tribunal will have to address is: 'In all the circumstances, and in the light of the information available to the employers at the time, was the conclusion that redundancies were necessary a reasonable decision for the employers to make?' It is irrelevant that later circumstances may show that the employer's expectations or forecasts were wrong: what is important is the state of the employer's knowledge at the time the redundancy decisions were made.

Cessation or diminution of the need for employees

The phrase in the statutory definition about the needs of the business for employees having 'ceased or diminished' covers situations in which either the whole or part of a workforce is no longer required. What is sometimes overlooked is the part of the definition that states that such cessation or diminution may be either permanent or temporary. The requirement to make redundancy payments when there is only a short-term dip in business activity cannot be evaded by dismissing the employees and at the same time offering re-engagement at a later date – unless the interval between dismissal and re-hire is not more than four weeks. For example:

> An employee worked in a brickworks that had to be shut down for repairs. He was dismissed when this closure took place, but was told he could resume his job when the brickworks re-opened. After 11 weeks, he found another job, just two weeks before the brickworks was due to re-open. He claimed a redundancy payment which his employers resisted – but they lost their case, because there had clearly been both a dismissal and a temporary business cessation of more than four weeks. (*Gemmell* v *Darngavill Brickworks*)

All, or part, of a business: the place of work

A 'business' – the term used in the legislation – is not restricted to commercial undertakings such as private-sector trading companies. It covers all employing organisations including, for example, local and health authorities, charities, and schools. A whole business may also include two or more associated businesses if they are under common ownership, or if one business owns or controls another. So in a potential redundancy situation, jobs and employment opportunities can be assessed for the group as a whole.

There are no great problems in interpreting the legislation if the whole organisation is closed down and all the employees are dismissed on redundancy grounds. More difficult situations may arise when the closure, or the diminution of requirements for employees, occurs in only part of a business. The statute refers to redundancy occurring in 'the place where the employee was employed'. What does 'the place' mean?

If all the organisation's activities and employees are located on one site, there is no distinction in this respect between a redundancy situation affecting all employees and one limited to just one part of the business – say, the stores within a factory. But many organisations have many sites, and if one is closed or reduces its workforce, there may still be a need (even an increased need) for the same type of work and employees on other sites. If the surplus employees on the closed or diminished site are dismissed, does this qualify as legally fair redundancy or should they have been transferred to fill any suitable vacancies on other sites? The question is particularly important when organisations relocate their activities – such as the move of an office from central to outer London or the provinces.

At one time, the courts decided questions of this kind solely by what was known as a contractual test. In other words, the place of work in any particular case was the place or places specified in the contract of employment. This did not create any problems if the contract specified one distinct location but did result in some unsatisfactory decisions where contracts included open-ended mobility clauses such as, for example, 'The company may at any time require you to transfer to any other location.' This type of clause was accepted as giving the employer a right to transfer an employee anywhere in the UK, regardless of personal circumstances and the pattern of previous employment. A refusal could be taken as a failure to obey a reasonable instruction – justifying a disciplinary dismissal rather than redundancy.

That position has now changed, based largely on a CA decision in a case involving peripatetic waitresses (*High Table* v *Horst*). The details of the case, which involved claims of unfair dismissal, are not of great significance. What is important is the CA's decision that the test of whether redundancy has occurred in a person's place of work should not be determined simply by the wording of a mobility clause. An employee's place of work, said the CA, had to be determined by looking at the factual circumstances. If an employee had in fact worked only in one place during his or her employment, the judges said it would defy common-sense to widen the concept of the place of work simply because of the existence of a mobility clause. The CA went on to say that it would be unfortunate if the way the law was interpreted encouraged the use of mobility clauses as a means of defeating genuine redundancy claims. This does not mean that all mobility clauses are useless. A mobility clause is still likely to be supported by the tribunals and courts if in fact the employee has moved from location to location – and probably, if this is not the case, if the extent of the mobility is clearly defined and, for all except senior managerial staff, relatively limited.

Organisations that have good operational reasons for preserving their right to move employees between locations should therefore use mobility clauses such as the following for the generality of their employees:

□ Your initial place of work will be our offices at...but you may also be required to work at our other site at . . . (*This assumes the second site is within reasonable daily travelling distance for the employees concerned.*)

□ You may be required to work at any site to which the company may relocate within a six-mile radius of Charing Cross. (*This assumes the present site is also within this defined area.*)

□ You will be employed to work on contracts at various of our clients' sites within reasonable daily travelling distance of our head office at . . . (*This type of clause may be suitable for such employees as office cleaners, building workers and contract catering staff.*)

The courts have recognised, however, that in some occupations, a mobility clause can be much more widely drafted. For example, civil engineers who work for large, national construction companies may well have a contractual clause stating they will work on any site in the UK. Their 'place of work' for redundancy purposes may then be taken as the UK as a whole – provided that in any individual case there is evidence that the person concerned has in fact moved around the country. So when work finishes on one contract in, say, Kent, and the engineers are posted to a new site in Cheshire, they cannot refuse the transfer and claim redundancy compensation.

In many relocation cases, there is no mobility clause in the contract of employment. Where there were disputes as to whether the move gave rise to redundancy, the courts used to consider whether there were any implied (ie unwritten) mobility conditions in the contracts. One case involved a building worker in Liverpool who had only ever worked within daily travelling distance of his home in the city. Work fell off and his company instructed him to work on a contract in Barrow, which would have required him to live away from home during the week. He refused to go, was dismissed, and then claimed redundancy compensation. The court decided that, based on custom and practice, there was an implied term in his contract that his place of work was within daily travelling distance, so he had in fact been made redundant. Interestingly, the same conclusion would almost certainly now be reached, despite the courts having abandoned the contract test. On the current basis of reaching a common-sense decision based on what has actually been happening, this man's place of work would be interpreted as where he has actually been working – within the environs of Liverpool.

There have been cases in the past involving senior managers without mobility clauses where the legal decision has been that employees such as managing directors have an implied contractual duty to work anywhere their organisation requires. With non-managerial employees, the trend was to accept that employers had an implied contractual right to transfer employees without a mobility clause to any new workplace within reasonable daily travelling distance of their homes. And this could mean that the distance involved in London might be greater than in a small provincial town – because lengthy daily commuting times are common for those working in the London area. Whether these views would still stand on the current, common-sense basis is conjectural: there have as yet been no leading cases involving employees without mobility clauses under the current approach. It seems likely, however, that the more senior the job, the wider the area would be within which an employer could reasonably expect the employee to relocate – especially if there was an adequate reimbursement of the costs of moving home.

A related issue is whether the employer acts reasonably in the way a legitimate mobility clause is acted on. In one case, an industrial tribunal decided that although the organisation concerned had a contractual right to require an employee to transfer to another distant location, it had acted unreasonably in giving the employee only one day's notice of the move. Good employers realise that a change of location that involves the employee in moving house (or living away from home) can be a cause of significant stress. It makes good sense to provide employees in this situation with every possible assistance – including adequate notice – rather than relying simply on the letter of the employment contract.

Diminution of the requirement for employees

Many redundancies result, not from the closure of whole businesses or workplaces, but from changes in the need for particular jobs. This is not just a matter of the volume of work of a particular kind diminishing and employees thereby becoming surplus to requirements – although that, indeed, is a very common form of redundancy. There are two other circumstances that meet the statutory criteria for redundancy; and both include situations in which the volume of work may not just be unchanged – it may even be increasing:

□ where employees are displaced by other means of getting the work done – such as by automation or by the replacement of employed staff by contractors

□ where, by reorganisation, new working methods, or simply employees working more productively, the same (or more) work can be performed by fewer employees.

At law, it is fair to dismiss employees on redundancy grounds in these situations, provided that the proper redundancy procedures are followed. The important point of definition and principle is that it is the employer's requirement for *employees* that determines the redundancy position. Whether the volume of work is diminishing, is constant or is even increasing is irrelevant. Consequently, it is both possible and not uncommon for legitimate redundancies to occur in successful, expanding organisations when, because of changes in the way work is organised (or in the nature of particular functions), they no longer have a need for a particular employee – although this is a point not always understood or readily accepted by the employees concerned.

Work of a particular kind

The statutory definition refers to a diminution or cessation of the needs of the business for employees to carry out 'work of a particular kind'. This phrase can cause difficulties, particularly when employees are dismissed following some change in their duties or conditions of service. The question then arises whether there has been a redundancy because the business no longer needs employees to do work of the original kind.

As with mobility clauses, the courts used at one time to apply a contract test to this question. The particular kind of work was held to be whatever kind of work the employee could be required to do within the contract of employment. This led to some odd results when very open-ended contractual terms were involved, such as a decision that a specialist music teacher was not redundant when a music department was closed because his standard teaching contract simply said he was employed to teach on whatever subjects the school required – and there was a vacancy for a woodwork instructor!

This contract test was rejected by the EAT in 1997 (*Safeway Stores* v *Burrell*). Returning to the words of the statute, the EAT said three questions had to be asked in establishing whether an employee was redundant:

- ☐ Was there a dismissal?
- ☐ Did the employer require fewer employees to carry out a particular kind of work?
- ☐ Was the dismissal caused wholly or mainly by this reduced requirement?

On this test, an employee doing one kind of work could be redundant if he or she was dismissed to make room for another employee doing a different kind of work in which fewer employees were required. In other words, this EAT decision made it legitimate to use what had become known as 'bumping' redundancies – dismissing employees in one job in which there was no reduction of requirement to provide work for otherwise surplus employees in another job. 'Particular kind of work' simply meant the work being done by employees who were no longer required.

However, in another case in 1998 (*Church* v *West Lancashire NHS Trust*), the EAT decided that unless a person is dismissed because there has been a reduction of the requirement for employees in the same kind of work, the dismissal cannot be for redundancy. In the case of an employee doing different work dismissed to make a job for an employee surplus in different work, the EAT said the dismissal was not caused by redundancy as defined by the statute but by the procedure the employer had chosen to follow in dealing with a potential redundancy. The question then was whether or not it was an unfair dismissal – not whether it was redundancy. This decision rules out bumping redundancies. Until a higher court resolves this matter, the legal status of such dismissals remains uncertain.

What is clear is that a strict contract test is not applicable, and the question in any specific case as to what constitutes the particular kind of work involved in the redundancy directly or indirectly will be assessed on a largely common-sense basis. In the main, this will involve looking at what the employees concerned actually do, have done, or could reasonably be expected to do as a normal part of their jobs.

It is also clear that dismissals resulting from changes of conditions of service (eg new pay rates, different hours of work) do not fall within the statutory definition of redundancy if the nature of the work remains unchanged. What must be considered is the extent to which, if at all, there has been a change in the kind of work, although this, too, can be a matter of judgement and therefore of potential dispute. How big a change must there be before the old and new work duties or activities are sufficiently different to be considered as different particular kinds of work? The implication of various cases is that there must be a significant change either in what the employee actually does or in the degree or range of skill or knowledge. For example, in a case involving the BBC, the EAT decided that the work of a Mark 2 (senior) radio producer was a different particular kind of work from that of a Mark 1 producer, even for the same subject area. Similarly, an earlier case had decided that the work of a heating engineer with plumbing skills was a different kind of work from that of a plumber with some heating skills.

The 'redundancy situation'

The term 'redundancy situation' is frequently used to describe the position an organisation finds itself in when it forecasts or experiences employee surpluses. It is a phrase that does not appear in the legislation but that can be the subject of misunderstanding, with adverse legal consequences. As Chapter 7 explains, there is a legal requirement to conduct formal consultations with recognised trade unions or elected employee representatives about impending redundancies. Managers sometimes treat this as a requirement to contact trade unions only after specific dismissal decisions have been made. Some trade union officials claim a right to consultation a long while in advance of such decisions, and whenever the first possibility of redundancy emerges. Managers and trade unions will describe their respective interpretations as applying when there is 'a redundancy situation'. Setting aside for the moment what constitutes good consultative practice, it is necessary to have a clear understanding of the implied legal definition of a redundancy situation in which consultation is prescribed.

The legislation describes the consultation requirements as coming into effect when 'the employer is proposing to dismiss as redundant' one or more employees. The Act prescribes certain time limits, dealt with in Chapter 7. The definitional point is that for statutory consultative purposes, a redundancy situation comes into existence only when forecasts or plans indicate the probable need to make redundancy dismissals.

Key points

□ Fair, effective and legally sound management of redundancy must be based on a clear understanding of the legal definition of redundancy, as set out in the relevant statutes and interpreted by the courts.

□ For a redundancy to occur, there must be a dismissal – either direct or implied.

□ If the fact of dismissal is disputed, the onus is on the employee to prove that a dismissal occurred.

□ If the reason for dismissal is disputed, the employee claiming it was for redundancy, the onus is on the employer to prove otherwise.

□ In a disputed case, an employment tribunal should decide only whether the reason for the dismissal was genuine redundancy as legally defined – not whether the redundancy was or was not necessary.

□ To qualify for statutory redundancy rights, the dismissal must be wholly or mainly attributable to the cessation of a business or part of a business (actual or intended), or to the actual or expected cessation or diminution of the requirements of the business for employees to carry out work of a particular kind in the place where they are employed.

☐ The change in the needs of the business for employees may be temporary or permanent.

☐ A 'business' may consist of a group of associated businesses.

☐ The employee's place of employment may be an actual single work location or the locations where the employee has been employed.

☐ It is the requirement of the business for employees that determines whether redundancy occurs – not the volume of work. Redundancies may occur when the amount of work to be done is static or expanding and the employer finds ways of getting this work done with fewer employees.

☐ 'Work of a particular kind' generally means work of a broadly similar nature, not necessarily identical work.

☐ If the non-statutory term 'redundancy situation' is applied to the circumstances in which the law requires formal collective consultation, it should be applied to a situation in which the employer has evolved proposals for the dismissal of employees on redundancy grounds.

5 HANDLING INDIVIDUAL REDUNDANCIES

However well an organisation has conducted its redundancy planning and produced redundancy procedures or agreements, the ultimate test of good management – and of compliance with statutory and case-law – is how individual employees who face redundancy dismissal are dealt with. The value of fair and objective redundancy selection criteria discussed in detail in the next chapter can also be lost if, in an individual instance, bias or undue haste occur in the actual selection and dismissal process. Beyond these legal implications, employee morale and the organisation's reputation can also suffer as a result of thoughtless or unsympathetic attitudes and practices on the part of individual managers who have the difficult task of telling employees about their redundancy selection. This chapter considers the subject from two viewpoints – the strictly legal, and that of good employment practice which extends into aspects not covered by legislation or case-law.

There are three principal elements to consider in relation to the law, and there are 'good practice' aspects to each:

□ notification and consultation
□ alternative employment
  – finding other work
  – offer and acceptance
  – trial periods
□ time off to find other work.

In addition to matters covered by statute and case-law, five other factors need to be addressed to ensure a high standard of management in the handling of individual redundancies:

☐ how to tell the bad news
☐ training managers to handle redundancies well
☐ training redeployed staff
☐ the compensation package – dealt with in Chapter 9
☐ redundancy counselling – the subject of Chapter 11.

Notification and consultation

There are no specific statutory requirements relating to the notification of redundancy to individual employees, or to consultation with employees as individuals.

Despite the absence of statutory provisions, employment tribunals and courts have placed a great deal of importance on individual consultation in deciding whether redundancy dismissals have been effected in a fair and reasonable manner.

The origin of this approach was the guidance provided by the Industrial Relations Code produced by the Advisory Conciliation and Arbitration Service (ACAS) in 1971. Parliamentary endorsement of this Code was withdrawn in 1991 as part of the government's general diminution of trade union rights. The Code, although not directly enforceable at law, was required to be taken into account by tribunals when considering the fairness or reasonableness of an employer's actions. In other words, it had a similar status in relation to employment legislation as the Highway Code has to statutory requirements about driving. In a section on redundancy, the Code recommended:

☐ warning any employees concerned of the likelihood of their being made redundant, and explaining the reasons
☐ providing an opportunity for these employees to respond, perhaps with alternative proposals
☐ inviting volunteers to be made redundant before implementing enforced redundancies
☐ giving consideration to alternative work, transfers and re-training
☐ the general provision of assistance to redundant employees.

The tribunals and courts adopted these points as factors to consider when assessing the fairness of disputed redundancies and, as a result, the principles have acquired (and retain) the force of law through case-law, even though the Code itself no longer exists.

Case-law does not make any specific distinction between notification and consultation – it simply expects some discussion to take place between an employer and a potentially redundant employee before a final redundancy decision is made. This discussion implies that the employer notifies the employee of the redundancy situation and of the reason that the employee has been selected. The employer should also notify the employee that he or she is able to respond. The EAT, commenting on the ACAS code in 1985, summarised its definition of consultation as:

> The joint examination and discussion of problems of concern to both management and employees, involving a search for mutually acceptable solutions through a genuine exchange of views and information.

The key principles were established by a House of Lords decision in 1988:

> Mr Polkey was one of four delivery van drivers. His employing company needed to cut its overheads and reorganised the work, replacing the four drivers with two van salesmen. Only one of the four drivers was considered suitable for these new jobs. The other three, including Mr Polkey, were called into the office and told they were being made redundant forthwith. Mr Polkey pursued a complaint of unfair redundancy dismissal, pointing to the complete absence of any prior warning or consultation. The company argued that even if they had consulted, it would have made no difference to the redundancy decisions. The industrial tribunal, although describing the manner of dismissal as 'a heartless disregard' of the ACAS code, agreed with the company's argument and said the dismissal was fair. The case was then appealed all the way to the House of Lords. The Lords decided in favour of Mr Polkey, saying that industrial tribunals should not address the hypothetical question as to whether or not the outcome would have been different if the correct procedure had been followed. Tribunals had to assess whether the employer acted reasonably at the time of dismissal – and a failure to consult would in almost every case be unreasonable. Only where the facts available to the employer at the time of

dismissal were so clear as to show that consultation 'would have been futile', might the absence of consultation avoid being judged unreasonable. (*Polkey* v *Dayton Services*)

A procedural flaw (a failure to consult) may thus convert an otherwise fair redundancy into an unfair dismissal. This may seem a rather legalistic approach, but closer consideration shows it to be supportive of good employment practice.

What it prevents is the tendency of some employers to assume they know what employees' reaction to redundancy would be, without actually asking them. Managers who resist or resent the obligation to consult often say they can see little point in talking to the employees who have been selected for redundancy – 'There's nothing they could say which would change the position.' On occasion, these managers may be right, but the Polkey decision says, in effect, you can't be sure unless you consult, and it is unreasonable not to do so. Consultation is therefore a key element in the sound management of redundancies. It provides a potentially redundant employee with the opportunity to put forward a variety of views that might alter the intention to dismiss. In particular:

☐ a willingness to accept a lower-paid or lower-status job which the employer might well have assumed was of no interest

☐ a query about the assessment (eg of competence or attendance) on which the selection has been based and perhaps the correction of an error in such assessment

☐ if the redundancy is caused primarily by the need to cut costs, a suggestion about an alternative way of saving an equivalent sum.

It is an extremely confident (not to say foolhardy) manager who would claim to know, without actually talking to an employee, what that employee might say about issues of these kinds.

Another important issue is how long consultation should last, and whether there should be an interval of time between the consultation and a decision to effect a redundancy dismissal. Is it sufficient, for example, for the whole process – notification, explanation, discussion of the employee's reaction, decision to dismiss – to occur during one 30-minute interview? Good practice indicates otherwise, and tribunal cases in which this question has been a feature certainly indicate that something more is needed. Both employee and employer need to have sufficient time to consider each other's views before a final decision is reached – the actual time suggested in these cases ranging from one and a half days to three weeks. In one case it became clear in less than two days that the employee concerned would neither accept a down-graded job nor work out his notice – so it was fair for the employer then to effect the redundancy. In other cases, a period of two to three weeks has been held reasonable to allow the employer and employee to consider various redundancy options. Note that the key issue is the time between first talking to the employee and the decision to dismiss – not the notice arrangements once a dismissal is decided.

The emphasis on genuine consultation conflicts with the not-uncommon practice among some employers of informing employees of their redundancy and terminating their employment at the same time, paying monies in lieu of notice. In extreme cases, keys to company cars are collected, taxis are arranged to take the dismissed employees home, and they are escorted from the premises by security staff. Two reasons are often given for abrupt dismissals of this kind:

☐ fear that disgruntled employees will be a disruptive influence if they stay to work out what, in some cases, may be quite lengthy notice periods

☐ concern that the loyalty of these employees in their access to and use of sensitive commercial information cannot be relied on once they have been given notice.

There can be circumstances in which both these considerations are valid. Some employees react very strongly to redundancy decisions, even when the employer has acted with impeccable fairness. There is a risk that they could cause problems by displaying an antagonistic attitude during their last few weeks at work. Similarly, a redundant employee working out notice who has access to pricing or contract information of significant value to a competitor with whom he or she is seeking another job may be tempted to use this information in a way that would damage the current employer. What are organisations to do in these circumstances?

The first step is to consider very carefully whether significant risks actually exist. It is all too easy to assume that problems will arise – really as an excuse to avoid consultation – when in reality the risks may be very slight. If there are real grounds for fear of disruptive behaviour, a two-stage process may be helpful:

☐ Start with a consultative discussion, explaining the proposed redundancy action but not effecting a dismissal. Close the discussion by saying 'We realise this must be a shock and we want to give you time to think it over and talk again before we make a final decision. We think it best if you now take a few days off to consider the position and come back to see us again next week' – making it clear that the employee should take immediate special paid leave (say, three to five days) and fixing an appointment for the next meeting.

☐ Listen to what the employee has to say at this next meeting and, if legitimate new issues are raised, alter the original redundancy proposal accordingly. But if nothing new is raised, or if the employee's suggestions cannot reasonably be accepted, explain that the dismissal decision will now have to go ahead. Explain the notice entitlement and encourage the employee to leave immediately by pointing out that non-contractual payments in lieu of notice have the advantage of being paid tax free, but leave open the option of working out the notice period. If the employee chooses the latter, but there is still genuine concern about his or her possibly disruptive behaviour, make it clear in a friendly but firm and unambiguous manner that normal working is expected, and that should there be cause for complaint about this, employment would have to be terminated before the end of the notice period. If necessary, point out that if the complaint was a very serious one (eg gross misconduct) this would prejudice the employee's right to a redundancy payment. (This point is explained in Chapter 9.)

Of course, if the employee makes it clear at either of these two interviews that he or she is unwilling to co-operate, it is not unreasonable to bring the consultation to an end and effect the redundancy dismissal with pay in lieu of notice.

The situation is more difficult if it is considered that there is a significant and serious risk of commercial damage through the employee's misuse of confidential business information. A procedure that still allows a delay between initial notification and the final decision is then to consult on a Friday afternoon, re-assemble on Monday, and make an immediate decision after that discussion. Security measures can be taken to ensure the employee has no access to the office over the weekend to extract sensitive documents.

Procedures of this kind should apply to only a very small minority of cases. Normally a much more supportive approach is needed, with consultation a very genuine opportunity for the employer to reconsider the proposed redundancy dismissal in the light of any comments and suggestions the employee may make. The way this process should be handled is discussed in the later section in this chapter on 'How to tell the bad news'.

Alternative employment

Finding other work

Once a redundancy decision has been made, it is essential for both good practice and legal reasons to explore the possibility of alternative employment. There are two main legal reasons why this is necessary:

☐ Employees are not redundant unless there is no available work for them – and this includes any work that they may reason-ably be required to do within their contracts of employment. Contracts are sometimes flexible, using phrases such as 'You may be required to transfer to any job appropriate to your skills, experience and grade level, in any part of the company'. This may well imply jobs with different job titles and in dif-ferent sections from the position in which redundancy occurs – so a thorough check must be made of current or impending vacancies across a possibly wide range of alternative work and job locations before the organisation can establish that a gen-uine redundancy situation exists. The first step must be to define the scope of the employee's contract – not to assume that the redundancy situation is limited to exactly the same job or jobs as the employee's current position. The question to resolve is: are there any vacancies anywhere in the organisa-tion for jobs that the employee could be required to do?

☐ Beyond this, case-law has made clear that an employer

should seek to find alternative work, 'so far as is reasonable'. In other words, although there is not a binding legal requirement to find and offer work beyond the scope of the employee's contract, a failure to act reasonably in this regard may make the dismissal procedurally unfair. The question to resolve is: are there any vacancies anywhere in the organisation that it would be reasonable to expect the employee to accept, even though he or she could not normally be required to do so?

With large organisations, a question that often arises is how widely across a multi-plant company or a multi-company group the employer should look for alternative work.

Each case needs to be looked at factually, rather than applying any general principle, although there is no doubt about the need to look for alternative work within the organisation that is the employee's contractual employer. The grey area is how far beyond this the search should extend if there are associated organisations. Managerial and legal decisions on this point will be influenced by such factors as the nature of the job and how closely the organisations concerned are linked or controlled.

In any individual case, the consultation discussion should help to establish the range of work that the employee might accept as suitable. This must involve looking at possible job opportunities in every department or unit of the organisation – not just in the department or section in which the redundant employee currently works. Some large organisations (eg multi-unit companies, local authorities) that have introduced extensive devolution of responsibility for personnel issues to line managers may have difficulty with this. But if they are to act responsibly towards their employees and avoid being faulted at law, they need to ensure all their managers understand that in a redundancy situation two policy considerations should apply:

☐ For redundancy purposes, the organisation must act as a corporate body and not as a collection of autonomous employing units.

☐ Therefore, potentially redundant employees anywhere in the organisation must have priority for appointment to suitable vacancies, wherever these vacancies may be.

The administrative arrangements to ensure these policies are applied may take several forms:

☐ Managers may be required to notify the central personnel department of potentially redundant employees, and that department will then carry out the necessary search for possible alternative work across all units.

☐ In the absence of a central function, any manager in whose unit redundancies are being planned may be required to circulate details of the employees concerned (and the nature of other work they might do) to all other units with a request for information about possible alternative work.

☐ On receipt of details of a potentially redundant employee in another unit (either from the personnel department or from another unit manager), and assuming a possibly suitable vacancy exists, a manager will be required to interview the employee to assess suitability before offering the job to any other person.

Suppose an alternative job becomes available just after a redundancy dismissal – does this make the redundancy unfair? The answer depends entirely on what the employer knew (or could reasonably have been expected to know) at the time of the dismissal. If the vacancy was unexpected (eg one caused by a sudden resignation) then the dismissal would not be unfair; but if the employer knew that a vacancy would shortly occur (eg one to be caused by a known, normal retirement), the dismissal might well be judged unfair.

Offer and acceptance

The objective should always be to make an offer of alternative employment, and if otherwise redundant employees accept offers of alternative employment, the law no longer treats them as redundant and, instead, counts employment as continuous – provided the following statutory conditions surrounding this offer and acceptance are met:

☐ The offer must be made and communicated to the employee before the current employment ends. This implies that the offer is made known to the employee during the notice period and before the last day of employment.

□ The alternative job must start either immediately the current job ceases or not later than four weeks afterwards. If current employment ends on a Friday, Saturday or Sunday, the four-week period counts from the following Monday – in other words, the weekend can be added to the strict four-week period.

□ If the terms and conditions of the new job differ from those of the previous job, there is a four-week trial period (see next section).

Offers can be made by 'associated employers' as well as by the employee's immediate employer. An associated employer is one controlling or controlled by the employing organisation, such as a fully or majority-owned subsidiary company, or a group holding company.

An employee who unreasonably turns down an offer of suitable alternative employment loses entitlement to the statutory redundancy payment, so, in a disputed case, the two issues of 'suitability' and 'reasonableness' have to be considered. The latter includes the reasonableness of the employer in making the offer, as well as that of the employee in rejecting it. Note that any offer of any new job, regardless of its nature, extinguishes the redundancy situation as soon as it is accepted. So an employee might well accept alternative employment which, if rejected, would have been judged unreasonable and unsuitable. This is not an argument for making apparently stupid offers on the off-chance that employees will accept them. It does reinforce, however, the value of discussing as wide a range of alternatives as possible during the consultation phase, as an employee might accept a much lower-paid or lower-status job than would generally be considered suitable.

Reasonableness

In a disputed case the 'reasonableness' to be considered includes that of the employer's offer, not simply that of the employee's rejection. This includes consideration of whether adequate information about the job was given to the employee.

An offer must provide sufficient information to enable the employee to make a sound and well-informed decision about its suitability. To quote an EAT judgment, the offer must 'embody important matters such as remuneration, status and job description'.

Where multiple redundancies are involved, employers do not always communicate information about alternative work individually with each employee, but rely on notices. For example, notices might be posted saying that any employee who is prepared to work at a new site will be employed there. Cases that have had to consider this type of collective offer indicate that the practice may meet the requirements of the statute – provided it is certain that all potentially redundant employees see the notices. One company fell foul of the law on this point when it was shown that an employee who was on sick leave had not seen the offer. It is, consequently, good practice to review the organisation's various employee information channels and ensure that those used will be seen by all the employees concerned. Many organisations are making increasing use of internal e-mail for purposes of this kind, in addition to the more traditional media of notice boards and newsletters. Ideally, however, employees should be notified individually, with particular care to include those away on sick or maternity leave, or on holiday.

So far as the employee's acceptance of an offer is concerned, there is no legal requirement for any formal or written procedure. Just saying yes and turning up for work are sufficient to indicate acceptance – although the prudent employer will ask for a signature of acceptance on a copy of the letter making the offer.

Care needs to be taken about the handling of an employee's refusal to consider an offer of any kind. It is not unknown for employees' immediate reaction on being informed about redundancy to be that they want to leave immediately and to show no interest in anything else the employer might offer. If, because of the employee's attitude, an available job is not offered, the employee retains the right to a redundancy payment. The only way of preventing this is to make the offer (preferably in writing) despite the employee's initial statement. Rejection may then be held to be unreasonable, and the right to a redundancy payment will be lost.

Once an offer has been made, its terms must be maintained. If the new job or its terms turn out in reality to be different, and less favourable, from how they were described in the offer, the employee is likely to be able to leave and claim the original redundancy payments. Cases of this kind have involved guarantees of overtime or bonus earnings not being met, the nature of the work being different, and benefits being withdrawn. There is no strict time-limit on the period after the new job has been started when issues of this kind can lead to justifiable resignations and claims for redundancy payments. The time-period can certainly extend beyond the statutory four weeks' trial, particularly if it takes longer to show, for example, that actual bonus or overtime earnings fell short of what had been promised.

Suitability

The question of an alternative job's suitability is subject to scrutiny by an employment tribunal only if an employee rejects an offer. There is no statutory definition of the word, other than the phrase 'suitable employment in relation to the employee'. Assessing suitability is consequently a matter for tribunals (and therefore employers) to consider on a case-by-case basis, looking not just at the job but also at the personal circumstances of the employee concerned. It is possible for the same job to be suitable for one employee but not another, as the following case shows:

> Two engineers both worked for the same civil engineering company. When work came to an end at one location – resulting in their potential redundancy – both were offered jobs at a site in the Hebrides. From there, they would be able to travel home in only one weekend in six. Both refused to accept the offers and claimed redundancy payments. The tribunal decided that, in general, this degree of job mobility (and the possibility of working a long distance from home) was normal in the industry, and in one case, a refusal was unreasonable. The other engineer, however, gave evidence that two of his five children and his wife were in poor health, and he needed to be readily available to help look after them. In his case, having regard to his domestic responsibilities, the tribunal decided his refusal of the offer was reasonable. (*MacGregor & MacCullum* v *William Tawse*)

Because suitability is a matter of judgment about facts – not about law – very few cases have been taken on appeal beyond the tribunals. There is consequently little binding case-law on the subject, because tribunal decisions do not constitute legally binding precedents and must therefore be treated merely as illustrative. The few cases that have been heard at higher appeal levels provide some guidance on the two key factors of pay and status, and indicate that pay preservation is not enough to make the offered jobs suitable – status may be of dominant importance. So a redundant head teacher who was offered but refused an ordinary teaching job as an alternative was held to have acted reasonably in rejecting this offer, even though the education authority had offered to continue paying a head teacher's salary. One or more of the following factors may be decisive, depending on the facts of each case:

- *Pay*. Any significant (though not minor) cut in pay (basic or earnings) is likely to make the offer unsuitable.
- *Status*. Any significant reduction in status – eg from staff to manual, or from senior to junior management – may also constitute unsuitability.
- *Nature of work*. The work needs to be of broadly the same character, or clearly within the employee's capability. A change from light assembly work to heavy manual operations might well be considered unsuitable, particularly for an older or less fit employee.
- *Working hours*. A major change, such as from day work to permanent or frequent night-shift working, might be considered unsuitable, particularly if the employee concerned had domestic responsibilities such as caring for children or an elderly relative.
- *Work location and home-to-work travel*. Another factor in which the employee's personal circumstances influence suitability. Regional variations may also apply, such as an acceptance of much longer daily travel times in London than elsewhere.
- *Nature of the industry*. Changes of job and work location may be considered normal in some industries (eg construction) but unusual and therefore unsuitable in others.

Although the law does not require offers of alternative employment to be in writing it is clearly good practice to confirm all offers by personal letter and ask for confirmation of acceptance by signature. Unless mass redundancies make it impracticable, it is also good practice to offer an opportunity for discussion about the offer. This discussion would generally benefit by taking place before the offer is finalised, but if this is difficult to arrange, an offer letter can be issued along the following lines:

> Following our recent discussion when we had to tell you that your job was being disbanded, we are now pleased to be able to offer you a suitable alternative appointment as a (*job title*) in the (*department/work unit*). The pay rate for this job is (*details*) and the working hours are (*details*). The other terms and conditions of service are the same as in your present contract. If you are willing to accept this offer, you should sign and return the enclosed copy of this letter, and report for work in the new job to (*name and location of person to report to*) at (*time*) on (*date*). Should you have any questions about this offer before deciding whether to accept, or if you feel you are not able to accept, please contact (*name*) who will arrange for a discussion. This is important as we cannot guarantee your entitlement to a redundancy payment should you decide not to accept this offer.
>
> If you accept, as we hope you will, your employment will continue without a break. You will also be entitled to a four-week trial period in the new job so that you and we can be sure the job is suitable.

A letter of this kind is suitable for vacancies that arise or are identified after redundancy notices have been issued. In many cases, however, an alternative job will have been found earlier, and can be discussed at the consultative stage. To pre-empt the situation that arises if an employee at that time says that no other jobs will be accepted (despite such work being available and despite the organisation's wish to keep the employee), it is as well to have an offer letter available at the time of the initial discussion, and hand it to the employee regardless of a negative attitude being taken. Only in this way can it be shown later that a suitable offer was made which was unreasonably refused.

Should an offer be refused, it is important to find out why before deciding to stop the redundancy payment, because there may be previously unknown personal or domestic reasons that would justify the refusal. This is best discussed, rather than being the subject of correspondence, and very careful consideration needs to be given to any reason related to personal difficulties in meeting the requirements of the new job. It is also essential that the employee understands the financial implication of rejecting an offer unreasonably, and this, too, is best explained by personal discussion.

Trial periods

It is sensible for both the employer and employee to have some time to discover whether a transfer to a new and different job is working out satisfactorily. A statutory trial period of four weeks in the new job comes into effect automatically whenever the terms and conditions are different from those of the original job. There does not have to be a formal notification of, or agreement to, the four-week trial. There is no trial period if the terms and conditions are the same – such as in a renewal of the contract because work has unexpectedly picked up after notice of redundancy was given and the job no longer needs to be disbanded. There may be other circumstances in which the new job and its terms differ – but not to an extent which would bring the trial period into play. There are then two factors to consider:

☐ If the differences are very minor or trivial, they may be discounted and no trial period applies.

☐ If the terms and conditions differ by being significantly better, they do count as differences – and so trigger the trial period. In other words, better jobs must be subject to a trial period, not just jobs with possibly less attractive features.

Trial periods start when the old contract ends and run for four calendar weeks. In one case, an employee argued that for the four weeks to include an 11-day Christmas and end-year shutdown prevented him from having a full four weeks' working experience, but the CA said the statute was unambiguous – four weeks was four consecutive calendar weeks, regardless of public holidays. In terms of good practice, however, it is obviously best to ensure that the working time provided for a trial period is adequate for both employer and employee to reach a sound conclusion about the suitability of the job. In cases where the statutory four weeks includes a holiday break, the sensible course of action is to agree an extension, although there is a potential problem. This is that the formal preservation of the employee's statutory right to a redundancy payment applies only during the strict four-calendar-week period, or for the duration of an extension only if this has been agreed specifically to provide for training. So if the extension cannot be described as being for training purposes, the good employer will nevertheless agree to pay at least the equivalent of the statutory compensation should the trial fail during the extended period.

The purpose of the trial period is to give the employer and employee a reasonable opportunity to assess whether the job is suitable. If either decides with good reason within the four weeks that it is not, and the employment is brought to an end either by resignation or dismissal, the employee must be treated as having been dismissed for redundancy when the original contract ended. Redundancy payments are then due.

An employee might decide the job is unsuitable for a variety of acceptable reasons, such as finding it too difficult, or too arduous, or too demanding in terms of travelling or working time. The employer might reasonably bring the trial period to an end because of the employee's evident lack of competence. Provided the reasons given by either employer or employee are connected with the job change (and are reasonable), the employee's entitlement to a redundancy payment for the termination of the original contract is preserved.

There are, however, two sets of circumstances in which a trial period is brought to an end and the employee loses an entitlement to a redundancy payment:

☐ if the employee leaves (or gives proper notice) during the trial period despite the job being suitable – in other words, acts unreasonably in leaving the job

☐ if the employer dismisses the employee during the trial period for a reason unconnected with the job change – eg for misconduct.

In trial-period cases involving disputes about the suitability of a job, or the reasonableness of the employee in leaving it, or the employer deciding the employee cannot do the job, employment tribunals have to apply a common-sense approach to what is 'suitable' and 'reasonable' in the circumstances. The same common-sense approach is dictated by considerations of good practice. Issues to consider are:

☐ Did the employee make a genuine attempt to make a success of the new job?

- Did the employer provide sufficient assistance to help the employee settle in?
- What were the principal reasons for the employee resigning or the employer dismissing? Were these genuinely related to real issues about the new job or the employee's personal circumstances?

The four-week trial period which preserves the employee's right to a statutory redundancy payment can be extended if the following conditions are met:

- The extension must be agreed in writing between the employer and employee before the new job starts.
- The extension must be specifically for a period of retraining – it cannot be just for a generalised view that the trial may need more time.
- The written agreement must specify the date on which the extended period will end.
- It must also specify the terms and conditions that will apply after the end of the trial period.

An extension agreement that meets these conditions will preserve the employee's right to a redundancy payment for the original job – subject to the standard provisos about the reasonableness of the employee or employer bringing the trial to an end. There is no statutory limit to the length of a retraining extension, although if a dispute arose about the legitimacy of a dismissal during such an extension it could well be necessary for the employee or employer to show that the extension had been for genuine retraining purposes.

It is also possible to have more than one trial period. The first job tried may not prove suitable but, instead of bringing employment to an end, the employer may offer a new trial period in a different job. There is no statutory limit to the number of four-week trial periods that can be strung together in this way – although each must be for a different job.

Although the law does not require the four-week trial period to be formally notified or agreed, it is a matter of good practice always to explain this period to employees when discussing or offering alternative work – and to confirm it in writing. Reassurance about the preservation of redundancy rights during this period often helps to persuade an employee whose self-confidence has been dealt a blow by redundancy to try a new job.

Similarly, if the employee resigns, or if it is decided that the trial is unsuccessful, a face-to-face discussion to explore and explain the reasons is highly desirable. An abrupt dismissal without explanation might well be judged as unfair (under general unfair dismissal legislation) if it is difficult to show that the reason was specifically related to the trial, while employees who fail in the new job deserve sympathetic and supportive treatment – not action that adds to any sense of inadequacy.

The objective of any trial period should be its success, and this implies some effort on the part of the supervisor or manager of the new job, as well as by the employee. The principles to apply are very similar to those of an effective induction programme. That is, there should be a planned introduction to the job, the workplace, and the employee's new colleagues, and a phased and carefully monitored training or instructional period in which the employee is shown how to perform every aspect of the new job in order to meet its output and quality requirements. Should it be considered that retraining will take longer than four weeks, it is essential that the longer period is specified and put into the written extension agreement. In any event, the use of a mentor might be considered (ie an experienced work colleague with the ability and willingness to help the employee adapt to the new job), whereas the immediate supervisor or manager has a major responsibility to provide on-the-job coaching and to assess progress.

A formal decision also needs to be made just before the trial period ends as to whether the employee has shown sufficient ability to continue in the job. If the personnel department has a responsibility for the general oversight of redundancy management, it may remind managers of the impending expiry of trial periods and ask for a short report and recommendation about continued employment. A manager who decides the employee is unsuitable shortly after the trial period has ended might involve the organisation in an unfair dismissal case – as the expiry of the trial period can be taken as implying a positive assessment of suitability.

Time off

An employee under notice of dismissal for redundancy has a statutory entitlement to a reasonable amount of paid time off during working hours to look for another job (or to arrange employment-related training), and this obviously amounts to good practice. Employees who are about to lose their jobs deserve all possible help in finding other employment. If an employer refuses to allow time off, or gives time off but on an unpaid basis, the employee can take a complaint to an employment tribunal – provided this is done within three months of the date on which the time off (or pay) was requested. There is no statutory definition of 'reasonable', so in any disputed case this is a matter for a tribunal to assess, taking a common-sense view of the facts.

There has been very little case-law about this issue, but the following points need to be kept in mind by managers asked for paid time off by the redundant staff:

□ The statutory right applies only to employees entitled to a statutory redundancy payment – ie those with at least two years' service.

□ The right applies only after formal notice of dismissal has been given. It cannot be claimed by employees at large simply on the basis of an organisation's preliminary and general announcement of the likelihood of redundancies.

□ The right exists even when an employee has, in the opinion of the employer, unreasonably refused an offer of suitable alternative employment.

□ There is no statutory requirement for the employee to provide the employer with evidence about interview appointments in order to be granted time off. Tribunals expect employee and employer to behave reasonably about this. Only if there is persuasive evidence that the employee is not genuinely seeking work is it safe for the employer to refuse time off or pay.

□ In assessing what constitutes reasonable time off, tribunals will probably take into account such factors as the effect of the employee's absence on the work of the organisation, how difficult it is for the employee to find other work, and whether the organisation provides any other assistance (such as career or outplacement counselling).

☐ Although the statute defines pay in terms of the hourly-rate equivalent of a week's pay (see Chapter 9 for a definition), this is not subject to the limitation on a week's pay which applies to the calculation of statutory redundancy payments.

☐ If a tribunal case is found against the employer, the maximum sum that can be awarded to the employee is only two-fifths of a week's pay – one reason, perhaps, why there have been so few cases.

In terms of good employment practice, managers should be as helpful as possible in granting time off. There may have to be restrictions on this if the employee's absence creates operational difficulties, but in general it is best to lean towards a generous rather than restrictive approach.

How to tell the bad news

Breaking the news of redundancy is one of the most difficult tasks personnel or line managers have to face. It is quite possible to handle this correctly within the law (by giving the right information at the right time) but to do so in an insensitive or confusing way which adds unnecessary stress to an already stressful situation.

There are three common faults in telling employees about their redundancy:

☐ to be extremely abrupt, and consequently give the impression that some fault lies with the employee. This is a failing of the manager who wants to get the whole unpleasant business over with as soon as possible.

☐ to be so circuitous in getting to the point that the employee becomes thoroughly confused and leaves the interview without a clear idea as to what has been said and what happens next. This approach is sometimes the result of fear that the employee will react angrily or emotionally, so an attempt is made to soften the impact of bad news by avoiding direct statements.

☐ to tell the employee far more than can be absorbed in one meeting. In addition to the basic information about the redundancy situation, the manager goes into great detail about compensation payments, pension options and other matters, most of which fails to register with an employee whose thinking is initially dominated by the single message that he or she stands to lose employment.

Managers should prepare for a redundancy interview, making sure they have available all the information that may be needed to answer questions the employee may ask, and deciding when and where the interview should best take place. Privacy is essential, because some employees do become upset and (both men and women) break down in tears or react with anger. They should not be put in a position in which they can be overheard by others or seen by onlookers leaving the interview in an upset state. An organisation with any sense of responsibility towards its employees should do everything possible to help those affected by redundancy maintain their dignity and avoid any situation that creates embarrassment or a sense of humiliation.

This does not mean that the bad news has to be relayed in a slow, piecemeal fashion in tones of apologetic sympathy. In most cases it is best to be clear, concise and direct: 'As you know, we have just lost our main contract and are having to reduce the staff. I am sorry to tell you that on the basis of our normal way of deciding who will have to leave, your job is one of those that we expect to have to make redundant by the end of next month.' It is important to be direct and open about the reasons for redundancies and the method of selection: employees will not readily accept a decision they do not understand but will respect the manager who is straightforward and positive.

Managers themselves need guidance on handling these interviews – just as they do for selection or disciplinary interviewing. If the redundancy programme is on a large scale, it is helpful to assemble all those managers who have to tell their staff, ensure they all explain the situation in the same way, and to advise them on the various reactions they are likely to experience from their staff. There are three types of situation that managers should be helped to cope with in particular:

☐ The employee who reacts emotionally should be allowed to display these emotions without interruption. The manager should remain calm, not show embarrassment and, above all, not try quickly to damp down the emotional response by saying things like 'Please don't get upset.'

☐ The angry employee should also be allowed to work off the anger, and the manager should not react to offensive statements or accusations made in the heat of the moment.

☐ At the other extreme, the employee who initially makes no response at all, maintaining a silent, stiff upper lip, can be helped by being encouraged to talk.

The first interview is generally not a good time to go into details about compensation payments and other administrative details. If the line manager has broken the bad news, it is often best to arrange for the employee then to see the personnel manager for an explanation of the whole termination and compensation process – with the details confirmed in an explanatory letter. At this meeting, information can also be given about further supportive action – the subject of Chapter 11.

Training managers

Most management training programmes include modules on the skills of selection and appraisal interviewing and on the handling of disciplinary issues. For the many organisations that cannot be sure about their ability to maintain their present levels or types of employment, a case can be made for adding to these standard personnel topics sessions on the application of the organisation's redundancy selection criteria and the conduct of redundancy interviews. The role-playing of redundancy interviews, after an initial scene-setting talk, can be as effective in this context as role-played appraisal and disciplinary interviews are in their fields.

But coaching managers in the handling of redundancy interviews does not meet all the training requirements. Broader-based management development programmes cover business planning and performance management, and within this broader context managers should be made aware of all the issues discussed in Chapters 2 and 3 about planning to avoid or reduce the incidence of redundancy. In particular, they should be encouraged to adopt flexible human resourcing strategies. Training about the need to plan ahead and to be prepared to manage situations in which there is a potential surplus of staff can be as important an aspect of human resource management as recruitment and selection.

The inclusion of all aspects of redundancy management (prevention as well as implementation) in management training programmes has become more important in recent years with the widespread introduction of managerial devolution. Many organisations that at one time made all human resourcing decisions centrally have devolved much of this responsibility to unit managers, so far more managers now make decisions about the nature and size of their own workforces. Although there are many reasons why devolved management systems are more effective than the traditional centralist approach, there are legal risks – particularly in relation to redundancy – if unit managers do not have adequate knowledge and skill to handle human resource issues well. The law does not recognise an organisation's internal business units or functional sections as separate employers, so flaws in managerial decision-making within one unit may result in the organisation as a corporate body being 'put in the dock'. The solution is not to centralise detailed decision-making, but to equip unit managers with the know-how and skills to undertake this aspect of their jobs with due regard to the law and to the standards the organisation as a whole wishes to maintain. Partly this can be achieved by the advice and guidance given to line managers by their personnel specialists. But this advice may not always be sought (or listened to) if the managers have not received sufficient training to recognise the significance of the guidance they receive and to acquire the personal skills they need to fulfil their managerial roles.

Training redeployed staff

The need to provide induction training for potentially redundant staff who have been redeployed to other jobs is sometimes overlooked, it being assumed that because the employees already know about the organisation that employs them they will have no difficulties in settling into new jobs within the same general employing environment. In reality, the change involved in transferring from one section to another and acquiring a new set of working colleagues can be as traumatic as a complete change of employer. Different sections or units often have their own, different cultural or attitudinal characteristics, while any change in the nature of the work also implies initial learning requirements.

This book is not the place for a detailed exposition of the principles of effective induction. What can be suggested, however, is that the organisation's standard induction procedures should be followed for redeployed staff, except for those elements that remain unchanged by the transfer – such as information about the pension scheme. Good induction programmes use a detailed checklist of issues to be covered, and this can be used to identify all those aspects of the job new to the redeployed employee. Managers and supervisors have a vital role to play here in doing all they can to help the transferred employee adjust quickly and happily to the new job – another point to include in management training programmes.

A wider issue is the retraining of displaced staff for wholly different work as one of the long-term measures to avoid redundancy. It has its application also in individual cases, and this adds emphasis to the need for and value of detailed discussion with each potentially redundant employee. It is all too easy to make assumptions about what alternative work an employee might have the aptitude to be trained for – but unless these possibilities are discussed there is a considerable risk of missing opportunities for other than obvious retraining. Here are two examples from the author's personal experience of managing redundancy:

A redundant office cleaner who retrained as an accounts clerk. In her spare time she had helped a neighbour run a small grocery store and had acquired useful practical experience of much of the paperwork involved with delivery notes, stock-lists and invoices. This was not known to the cleaning supervisor and was discovered only in the course of a redundancy counselling discussion.

A redundant civil engineer who retrained as a personnel officer. An outplacement discussion about his interests and personal skills indicated he was far better suited to such work as personnel management than to what had been a not very successful technical career. He was willing to take a drop in salary to switch to a job as a personnel and training assistant in parallel with enrolment on a part-time course of study for relevant qualifications at the local college.

Of course, fundamental retraining of the kind typified in these examples is not always practicable. Vacancies may not exist, or there may be difficulties with the costs involved. Commonly, however, the barriers to assisting redundant employees make major career changes are more procedural (such as adherence to rigid age limits for trainees) or attitudinal. Even where cost is a significant element, too little account may be taken of the offset savings on recruitment and redundancy compensation, while managers and employees themselves may have too stereotyped a perception of what constitutes a normal or successful employee for any particular kind of work. Anecdotal evidence indicates that there is far more scope for retraining than actually occurs in many organisations.

Key points

- Consultation with individual redundant employees is a matter of good employment practice. It is also an important legal requirement established by case-law (not by statute).
- Consultation involves the employer in giving the employee adequate information about impending redundancy and giving serious consideration to any response the employee may make before a final dismissal decision is made.
- A redundancy dismissal may be fair in terms of its reasons and selection criteria, but unfair if the dismissal procedure is flawed – eg by omitting to consult.
- Managers should not omit consultation and dismiss instantly simply because they fear the employee may become disruptive.
- The principles of good employment practice and case-law require employers to take reasonable steps to look for alternative work before effecting redundancy dismissals. A failure to do so may make an otherwise satisfactory redundancy unfair.
- Alternative work can be any work that the employee is willing to accept, not necessarily work very similar to that of the redundant job.
- Large organisations should act corporately, not as a collection of autonomous units, in finding and offering alternative work.

- [ ] To meet statutory requirements and so avoid redundancy payments an offer has to be made before the current employment ends, and the new job must start immediately or within four weeks of the old job ending.

- [ ] An employee who unreasonably rejects a suitable offer loses entitlement to statutory redundancy payments.

- [ ] The suitability of an offer is a matter, in disputed cases, for tribunals to assess on the facts. A common-sense approach is needed.

- [ ] Suitability includes consideration of the employee's personal circumstances, such as travel difficulties or domestic responsibilities. The same offer may be suitable for one employee but unsuitable for another.

- [ ] Factors that may affect suitability include pay, status, the nature of the work, working hours, work location, and the normal characteristics of work in the particular industry.

- [ ] It is advisable to make offers of alternative work in writing, even though this is not strictly necessary in legal terms.

- [ ] If an offer is refused, the reasons should be sought before assuming redundancy payments can be stopped.

- [ ] Unless there is no change in the contractual conditions, all alternative work carries a statutory entitlement to a four-week trial period.

- [ ] The employee's entitlement to a redundancy payment is preserved during the trial period if there is a resignation or dismissal for reasons connected with the trial (ie either party deciding on reasonable grounds that the job is, after all, unsuitable).

- [ ] The entitlement to a redundancy payment is lost if the employee resigns for other reasons, or the employer dismisses for reasons unconnected with the trial (eg for misconduct).

- [ ] The four-week trial period can be extended by written agreement, made before the period starts, solely for the purpose of providing sufficient time for retraining.

- [ ] Any number of trial periods can be arranged, provided they follow each other without a break, as the employee is tried out in one job after another.

- It is good practice to give employees a written explanation of the trial period; to provide support and coaching during the trial; to monitor progress; and to make a formal decision about continued employment before the trial period ends.
- Employees have a statutory right to a reasonable amount of paid time off to look for other work during their period of notice.
- This right to time off exists even if an employee rejects the employer's offer of alternative work.
- Any redundancy interviews should be held in privacy.
- Angry or emotional employees should be allowed to express their feelings, and the manager should remain calm and positive.
- It is inappropriate to give a mass of detailed information about compensation and other administrative matters while employees are still absorbing the initial news of redundancy.
- Managers should receive training in all aspects of redundancy management – prevention and implementation – including particularly the handling of redundancy interviews.
- Redeployed employees require induction-type training to help them adjust quickly and successfully to their new jobs.
- Consideration should also be given to the possibility of displaced staff being retrained for wholly different work, and this necessitates counselling discussions that include long-term career issues.

6 SELECTING EMPLOYEES FOR REDUNDANCY

There are some circumstances in which the question of redundancy selection does not arise. A whole organisation may be closed, with job losses for all its people, or a single, specialist job may be disbanded. But whether a redundancy situation involves just one employee or many, there is often a need to select the person or persons whose employment is to end. For example, the introduction of new technology may reduce the number of jobs needed in a large payroll section by, say, 25 per cent – so which of the current employees is surplus? In an individual case, the single job being disbanded may be of a type – such as a manager's secretary – held by several other employees. In these circumstances, should the redundant employee be the person in the disbanded job or should someone else doing the same work elsewhere be made redundant? The way in which employees are selected for redundancy where there are choices to be made is a very major element of redundancy management that has important good-practice and legal aspects.

There are often misconceptions about this subject. For example, some managers and shop stewards mistakenly think that the law requires the 'last in, first out' method to be used. Selection for redundancy is a very relevant issue in the context of the subject of the last chapter – the handling of individual redundancies. The first response of many employees when first told about their redundancy is 'Why me?', and there have been many tribunal cases in which employees have complained of bias in the way they have been selected. Redundancies may also be challenged because of the way the selection process has been handled – for example, by failing to explain why certain factors are used, or by too rigid an application of the selection criteria.

There are two overlapping reasons for ensuring that an equitable and reasonable approach is adopted: to ensure compliance with the law and so avoid the financial penalties resulting from breaches of legal requirements; and to maintain a high standard of employee management and so retain the confidence of the workforce and maintain the organisation's reputation as a good employer. The baseline has to be compliance with the law, and this involves consideration of the following issues:

- genuine redundancy
- unfair redundancy
- unreasonable redundancy
- good and bad selection criteria
- employees' remedies.

Is the redundancy genuine?

The law recognises redundancy as a potentially fair reason for dismissal, but an employer cannot defend a case of unfair dismissal simply by claiming that the reason was redundancy. In such a case, the employment tribunal needs to assure itself that there has been a genuine redundancy. Attempts have been made from time to time to challenge redundancies in tribunals on the grounds that it was not necessary for the employer to have taken such action. For example:

A furniture company decided to close a factory which, in the judgment of the management, was no longer financially viable. Some of the employees made redundant by this decision sought to challenge their dismissals by arguing, in effect, that the redundancy was not genuine because the company's analysis of the commercial situation was faulty. The EAT ruled against the employees, saying that the courts had no jurisdiction to assess the reasonableness or wisdom of commercial decisions. Those were matters for the company. The remit of tribunals in these circumstances was simply to decide whether the company genuinely considered the factory closure was necessary, not to substitute their assessment of the commercial situation for that of the company's management. (*Moon* v *Homeworthy Furniture*)

Tribunals have only to decide whether the decision to effect redundancies is genuine, not whether it is wise. However, proving a redundancy is genuine (if this is challenged at a tribunal) does normally involve the employer providing evidence of the reasons for the decision, and this may well include showing the tribunal details of such commercial matters as declining order books, company losses, or a failure to retain a major customer.

Consequently it is advisable to be extremely clear about the reason or reasons for a redundancy situation, and to have sufficient evidence (particularly in documented form) to be able to explain the situation to a tribunal in the event of a redundancy dismissal being challenged. In some cases this might include summaries of changes in work volume or copies of letters from customers withdrawing their business. But redundancies can also result from changes in technology, managerial reorganisations and geographical relocation. Whatever the reason, a succinct explanation by a senior management witness, supported by whatever principal documents are relevant, will in most cases convince a tribunal that the decision to effect redundancies was based on a genuine assessment of the reduced need for employees to do work 'of a particular kind'. It is of equal importance to be able to explain to employees, their representatives and trade unions why redundancies are considered unavoidable. A failure to do so can generate suspicion about the motives involved – for example, suspicion that the aim is to get rid of difficult employees – or sap the workforce's confidence in their management's business competence.

Unfair redundancy

Proving that the redundancy was genuine does not, in isolation, prove the fairness of a redundancy dismissal. The legislation provides a clear definition of the circumstances in which an individual redundancy may nevertheless be unfair. This is when:

☐ the circumstances causing the redundancy of the dismissed employee apply equally to one or more other employees in

the same undertaking, in similar positions to the redundant employee who have however not been dismissed
- [ ] the reasons for selection relate to pregnancy or maternity
- [ ] the reasons relate to an employee's lawful actions or activities under health and safety legislation
- [ ] the employee is selected because he or she refuses to work on Sundays
- [ ] the reasons relate to the employee's membership or non-membership of a trade union or to his or her legitimate trade-union activities, or his or her role as an elected employee representative
- [ ] asserting a statutory right (eg the right to paid time off)
- [ ] acting as a trustee of a pension scheme.

NB: the above list has been extended by both the National Minimum Wage Act 1998 and the Public Interest Disclosure Act 1998.

There are a number of elements in the statutory definition that require more explanation:

- [ ] What is an 'undertaking'?
- [ ] What constitutes 'similar positions'?
- [ ] What trade union reasons make a redundancy unfair?
- [ ] What factors relating to pregnancy make a redundancy unfair?

Undertakings

The statutory definition of unfair redundancy has a *comparative* element – the difference of treatment between the redundant employee and others who could have been considered for redundancy. The argument of an employee complaining of unfair redundancy is, in effect, that if fair and proper selection criteria had been used, someone else would have been made redundant. This someone else must be employed 'in the same undertaking'. What is an undertaking?

There is no definition of undertaking in the statute, and the courts therefore assess each case on its own facts. There is no problem, of course, if the organisation has only one location or is a single organisational entity, but the issue can be important if there are several separate organisational units (eg factories, depots, departments, commercial divisions and the like). How widely may comparisons then be drawn?

The factors that have led tribunals and courts to classify different organisational units as being in the same undertaking include:

☐ common ownership

☐ common management – for example, two factories both the responsibility of the same production director

☐ common terms and conditions of employment

☐ similar functions or activities.

It should therefore be assumed that if there is any question about the fair selection of an employee in one location or organisational unit compared with another employee somewhere else, a tribunal would examine this from a common-sense, rather than highly legalistic, viewpoint. The test question is probably 'Would the organisation's need for a redundancy have been met by the redundancy dismissal of the other person?' An affirmative answer does not imply the other person should necessarily have been selected (because other facts also have to be considered) but it does indicate that the term 'undertaking' covers both employees. This is another example of the need to manage redundancies on a corporate basis, looking across the organisation as a whole and not delegating final redundancy decisions to the managers of individual departments or units.

Similar positions – the 'pool'

This is a related matter, although it introduces a concept that is not in the statute but has been developed by case-law – the 'pool' of employees from which redundancy selections were or could have been made.

Employers sometimes restrict this pool to the particular section or unit directly affected by the reduction in requirements for employees, despite the existence of other sections in which employees are doing the same or very similar jobs. They feel it would be unfair to inflict redundancies on employees outside the section directly concerned. But the redundant employees may then argue that it was unfair to use so restricted a pool.

The fundamental issue is whether employees are in 'similar positions'. Legal decisions about the meaning of this term have been somewhat confusing, although in general the various case rulings suggest a close similarity between 'work of a particular kind' (in the general redundancy definition) and 'similar positions'. For example:

> A transport company operated two types of lorries – articulated vehicles and smaller four-wheel lorries. Drivers of the articulated lorries had to hold Class 1 HGV licences; the other drivers needed only Class 3 licences, which did not cover the driving of articulated vehicles. The company reduced its articulated fleet and made Class 1 drivers redundant. There was a 'last in, first out' agreement, and the Class 1 drivers argued that this should have been applied to a pool that included the Class 3 drivers, some of whom had shorter service. The EAT disagreed, holding that the Class 1 drivers had different, not similar, positions from the Class 3 employees. (*Powers* v *A. Clarke & Co.*)

Other cases have made it clear that the fact that two employees may have the same job title does not in itself establish that they are in similar positions. What matters is the nature of their work – and the same job titles sometimes conceal major differences in duties and responsibilities.

In practice, the approach adopted to decide the size and nature of the pool from which redundancies are to be selected is best influenced by two principles:

□ to take a wide, rather than a restrictive, view of the pool, taking in other relevant units or sections than that in which the redundancy is proposed.

□ to interpret 'similar positions' as being jobs of a very similar, although not necessarily, identical nature, and which the employees concerned could quite naturally be required to undertake.

There will, however, always be an element of judgment needed as to whether the redundancy dismissal of someone in a similar position but not directly affected – in order to create a vacancy for an employee whose job is being disbanded – will be perceived by those concerned (and their colleagues) as unfair. What may affect this in some cases is the extent to which the organisation's published or agreed redundancy procedures specifies that this type of action will be taken.

Agreed redundancy procedures

Redundancy agreements negotiated with trade unions often include provisions specifying the selection criteria the organisation will use if redundancies become unavoidable. At one time, the law stated that any breach of such agreed criteria was automatically unfair. That is no longer the case, although breaking such a collective agreement would not conform to good management practice. It is quite possible, however, that the collective agreement has been incorporated into employees' individual contracts of employment. If this is so, and the employer departs from the agreed selection criteria, the employees then made redundant may be able individually to take legal action for breach of contract, as a 1998 case decided by the Scottish Court of Session illustrates:

> An employee worked for a company that had a redundancy agreement with its trade unions and was selected for redundancy. The collective agreement stated that selection for redundancy would be on the basis of 'last in, first out' – widely known as LIFO. Under LIFO, the employee would not have been selected. He argued that the terms of the agreement had been incorporated into his individual contract by the words used in his statement of terms and conditions. He therefore sought an interdict ('injunction' in English legal terminology) preventing the employer using the non-LIFO selection criteria – which the Court of Session granted. (*Anderson* v *Pringle of Scotland*)

Three points are worth comment. First, it is undesirable to break a collective agreement. Second, it is always worth checking whether or not such an agreement has been formally incorporated into individual employment contracts by the way employees' terms and conditions of employment have been defined. And third, collective agreements should be reviewed from time to time and, if necessary, re-negotiated to prevent their terms becoming outdated and unsuitable.

There are three sensible courses of action:

☐ Conclude a redundancy agreement with the trade union(s) which includes details of the agreed selection criteria; ensure the terms of this agreement are followed in practice; and re-negotiate these terms if circumstances indicate changes are desirable.

☐ In a non-unionised organisation, decide what criteria should be used; inform all managers accordingly; and ensure their consistent application of these criteria.

☐ If it is considered unwise to tie the organisation to one particular set of criteria, include in the trade union agreement, or in the organisation's own redundancy policy, a statement to the following effect:

> Should it become necessary at any time to select employees for redundancy, fair and reasonable criteria will be agreed (or determined) at that time. Selection criteria may thus vary from time to time in the light of the specific characteristics and business requirements of each redundancy situation.

Trade union basis for selection

Some employers have been tempted to use a redundancy situation as an opportunity to get rid of an active shop steward or even to reduce the level of union membership among the workforce by discriminating in the selection process against union members. The legislation states that redundancy dismissals of this kind are unfair – and imposes financial penalties accordingly.

There are two parts to this legislation. Firstly, there is the general reference to using trade union membership or activity as a basis for selecting for redundancy. Secondly, a detailed definition of these reasons is set out in the section of ERA dealing generally with unfair dismissal. This says that a dismissal – whether or not for redundancy – is unfair if the reason or principal reason is because the employee:

☐ was, or proposed to become, a member of a trade union

☐ took part, or proposed to take part, in trade union activities 'at an appropriate time'

☐ was not a trade union member, or refused to become one, or proposed to give up trade union membership.

Any possible exceptions to this general rule of unfairness, such as selecting a shop steward for a past record of breaking procedure agreements, need to be treated with considerable caution, and it would be unwise, as well as a highly questionable employment practice, to approach redundancy selection with a view to using it to resolve industrial relations problems. These are best dealt with directly. If a shop steward or union member frequently acts in breach of agreed procedures or continually behaves in a disruptive way, the most effective action would normally be to discuss the matter with senior union officials, apply the organisation's disciplinary procedure, give written warnings, and eventually dismiss on disciplinary, not redundancy, grounds if the conduct is not corrected.

Pregnancy and redundancy

Selecting a woman for redundancy because she is pregnant, or for any reason connected with pregnancy, is automatically unfair. This does not mean that a pregnant employee, or an employee absent on maternity leave, cannot be made redundant. If the reason for her selection meets the statutory redundancy criteria, her redundancy dismissal will be fair. What is unfair is to use pregnancy or a related factor as a reason for the woman's selection. The leading case on this subject illustrates the principles involved:

> Four YTS supervisors were on a scheme that had to be wound up and replaced by another scheme for which only three supervisors were required. The four supervisors were invited to apply for the three new posts and were told that any unsuccessful applicant would be entitled to a redundancy payment. One application was rejected specifically because the employee was pregnant and would need to take several weeks' maternity leave shortly after the new posts were established. She consequently made a complaint of unfair dismissal. The case went all the way to the House of Lords, who found in her favour. Their Lordships stated that any inconvenience caused to the employer by having to make arrangements for maternity cover were 'the price the employer had to pay as part of the social and legal recognition of the equal status of women in the workplace'. (*Brown* v *Stockton-on-Tees Borough Council*)

The message from this case is very clear: there are no circumstances in which any actual or anticipated inconvenience caused by pregnancy or maternity leave can be used as a reason for selecting a woman for redundancy. It must also be recognised that if a woman is properly made redundant during her maternity leave (eg because her job has been disbanded) she retains the standard right to be considered for suitable alternative employment which would be available on the date she is due to return to work.

Unreasonable redundancy

Redundancy dismissals are subject to the same test of reasonableness as are all other dismissals, this requirement being derived from the general provisions relating to unfair dismissal. When a redundancy is processed in accordance with an agreed procedure, the employer is unlikely to be judged to have acted unreasonably, but reasonableness can be a significant issue when no such standing practices exist. There has been a degree of ambiguity in the way this factor has been dealt with in case-law. In 1982 the EAT said that the question to consider was whether a disputed redundancy dismissal lay within the range of conduct that a reasonable employer could have adopted, and went on to suggest four guidelines:

- ☐ whether the selection criteria were chosen objectively and applied fairly
- ☐ whether employees were warned of, and consulted about, the impending redundancies
- ☐ if there was a recognised union, whether the union's view was sought
- ☐ whether adequate consideration was given to the availability of alternative work.

Employment tribunals then began to test redundancies against these four points, only to have the EAT state that the points were only guidelines and that non-compliance did not necessarily lead to a conclusion of unreasonableness. It all depended on the facts of each case. However, the first of the four points is certainly still of major importance in considering whether an employer acted reasonably. A case illustrates this:

> Employees in a meat-processing plant challenged the criterion the company said had been used in redundancy selection, not on the basis that it was in contravention of an agreed procedure or previous practice, but on grounds of its subjectivity. The company's

stated selection (or rather retention) criterion was to keep in employment 'those employees best suited to the needs of the business under the new operating conditions'. No supporting, objective factors were used – the company had merely made a list of employees and written 'yes' or 'no' against each name. An industrial tribunal refused to accept this as a fair and objective method of selection. (*Smith* v *Haverhill Meat Products*)

The third point is really covered by the trade union consultation requirements explained in Chapter 7. The second and fourth points – individual consultation and alternative job offers – are dealt with in Chapter 5.

Reasonableness is very much a matter relating to the whole redundancy process, not just to the particular facts about employee numbers and selection principles. Although the four EAT guidelines described above do not carry the force of law, they remain a useful set of reminders about the characteristics of reasonable redundancy procedures. Whether in the form of a collective agreement or in an organisation's policy and procedure manual, it is advisable to establish a fair process to be followed. Merely specifying selection criteria will not ensure that those criteria are always applied in a reasonable manner. If redundancy selection is delegated to individual line managers, it is essential that they are briefed fully about these criteria, how to apply them, and the requirements relating to individual and collective consultation.

Good and bad selection criteria

It is useful to list the criteria most commonly used and comment on the extent to which they meet (or fail to meet) the tests of fairness and reasonableness. They can be considered under the following headings:

☐ length of service

☐ age

☐ competence

☐ conduct

☐ attitude

☐ attendance

☐ health

☐ part-timers

☐ multiple criteria

☐ indirectly discriminatory criteria.

Length of service

'Last in, first out' is so common a selection criterion it has acquired a recognised acronym – LIFO. For many years, in many industries, it was the standard and often sole method of selection endorsed by collective redundancy agreements. It had the virtue of appearing to be impersonal, impartial and objective, and of being extremely simple to apply. Once the relevant pool of employees had been identified, a quick check on starting dates soon produced a list of employees in date order, and the names of those to be made redundant could be identified by drawing a line under the required number down from the top. LIFO has also been accepted by tribunals and courts as an intrinsically fair method.

From a management viewpoint, however, LIFO has some significant disadvantages – in particular, it takes no account of differences of competence between employees. Many redundancies occur when companies are trying to improve their effectiveness, but LIFO can result in the loss of highly skilled staff and the retention of others whose skills have not kept pace with the rate of technological change. In addition, many managers understandably take the view that if the workforce has to be reduced, employees who have displayed loyalty, reliability and commitment should be given priority over those whose attitudes or attendance have not been so satisfactory. LIFO is also a poor method of selection if the employees in a small group have similar and quite lengthy service. There is very little fairness in selecting an employee with service of, say, 12 years 3 months instead of a colleague with 12 years 4 months, simply because of this insignificant difference in length of service.

Although case-law gives strong support to LIFO as a fair and reasonable criterion, it does not go so far as insisting that length of service should always take priority over other factors. For example:

A car company used a combination of service and skills in their redundancy selection, with the particular aim of retaining a

workforce with the right balance of occupational skills and experience. Because of the skills factor, one employee was made
redundant who had longer service than others in his section. The
industrial tribunal thought his selection was unfair, reasoning
that his shortfall in skills should not have outweighed a priority
in length of service. On the company's appeal, the EAT reversed
the tribunal's decision, ruling that service did not necessarily
have to outweigh other important factors for which there was
good reason. (*BL Cars* v *Lewis*)

Against this, there have been a few cases in which the tribunals
or EAT have faulted an employer's selection method where
length of service appeared to have been given no consideration.
In cases of this kind the rulings have generally indicated that
service should have been included as one of the factors to be
used in selection, not that service alone should have decided
who went and who stayed.

Age

In the absence at present of any UK legislation against age discrimination, it might appear that age could be used as another
simple selection criterion. It would, however, have similar disadvantages to LIFO, because it could well lead to the redundancy
of highly competent staff and the retention of less capable or less
experienced employees. It would also be a criterion far less likely
to find favour with trade unions, for it would generally discrim-
inate against employees with long service. In short, using age
does not seem fair. Great care would also need to be taken to
guard against the possibility that age criteria would constitute
indirect sex discrimination. If there was a preponderance of one
sex in the targeted age group, and this differed from the gender
profile of the retained employees, a case for indirect discrimination might well be established. Using age as a general criterion
would also be contrary to the government's code of practice on
age discrimination.

There is, though, an important exception: the selection for
redundancy of employees near, at, or above normal retiring age.
Making employees redundant who have reached the normal
retirement age for their organisation (or who are aged 65 or over)
is not subject to potential legal challenge, because employees in
that age range are at present statutorily barred from initiating

complaints about redundancy selection or payments. Moreover, their selection may well be urged by the trade unions. The situation is not as clear-cut for those below, but near, retirement age. This is a matter of judgment and common sense. Thus, to select those within two years of retirement may well be accepted as reasonable, but to extend this to employees with as many as 10 years to go would be far more questionable – on managerial, moral and legal grounds. No hard and fast age level can be suggested, because in any disputed case many other factors specific to the circumstances would probably need to be examined.

Competence

Selection on the grounds of skill, experience or competence is accepted by the tribunals as a potentially fair criterion. It is also the method most favoured by employers, because it clearly makes a great deal of sense to keep those employees who are most valuable to the organisation and to let go the less skilled. It might almost be described as a criterion for retention, for the start of the process may well be to produce a list of those employees whose continued employment is considered essential. However, to be fair in practice as well as in principle this method must not be applied casually. The differences in skill or competence that result in some employees staying and others being made redundant need to be clearly defined and objectively assessed. So an employer in one case who selected employees on the basis of retaining those who 'would keep the company viable' was held to have acted unfairly. The criterion, although vaguely related to competence, was far too subjective in its application. Consequently, it is not good enough to say that selection was based on differences in competence but then to be unable to explain what these differences were. Objective factors must be used, and these may include:

☐ professional or occupational qualifications – provided these are relevant to the type of work or the needs of the business

☐ specific work skills or experience – with the same proviso as for qualifications

☐ completion of specific skills-training courses or modules – internal or external (ie the better-trained employees are retained)

☐ performance appraisal records that record objectively assessed differences in performance standards

☐ competence assessments produced through any thorough and objective system.

Conduct

Conduct is another commonly used factor, usually taking employees' disciplinary records into account. For example, it might be decided that any employee who is currently under a formal written warning (or who is on a final warning) will be selected for redundancy before employees with clean disciplinary records. It would appear from cases in which conduct has been a factor that a conduct criterion is potentially acceptable, but that great care is needed in how it is applied. It carries a particular risk of confusing the difference between disciplinary and redundancy dismissals and of giving employees at large the impression that redundancy itself is a quasi-disciplinary measure.

Like other factors, an employee's disciplinary record is generally best considered as only one of the factors that may be taken into account, and only in extreme cases should it be treated as the sole basis of redundancy selection. For example, it would probably be accepted as fair, when only one employee has to be made redundant, to select an employee who is on a final warning if the only other possible choice is a colleague with broadly the same service and experience and a good conduct record. On the other hand, to dismiss an experienced long-service employee with a two-year-old first warning when other possibilities included an inexperienced recent recruit could well be judged unfair.

Attitude

It is not uncommon for employers to consider qualitative factors such as co-operativeness or commitment as redundancy selection criteria. This takes the assessment of individuals into a more subjective area than the facts about disciplinary records, because distinctions may have to be drawn on attitudinal factors between employees who all have generally satisfactory records of conduct. While there is clearly some logic in taking account of such issues as an employee's past willingness to work overtime, to volunteer to do unpleasant tasks or to take initiatives in making job improvements, there is also a risk of such generalised factors as 'commitment' being interpreted differently by different managers or applied differently by the same manager to different employees. Personality likes and dislikes can very easily be rationalised into apparently impersonal assessments of such imprecise behavioural characteristics.

The intention may thus be fair, but the application unfair. An example might be the use as a criterion of a generalised concept of 'merit' – potentially fair – but failing to define in objective terms how this is to be assessed and applied. If criteria of this kind are used, they need definition or at least illustrative examples to show the basis of assessment. Certainly, in any disputed case in which an employee was selected because of a lower level of commitment than another, a tribunal would expect to hear evidence of events or incidents that led to the different assessments.

Attendance

There have been differences of view in case-law about the fairness of attendance records as the sole selection criterion. In some cases, a strict application of predetermined attendance standards, without attention being given to the reasons for absences, has been ruled unfair. In others, the view has been taken that the reasons are immaterial – poor attendance is poor attendance. There has been much more agreement, however, about the need for any attendance records to cover a reasonable time period. For example:

> A vehicle manufacturer assessed attendance by reference to the six-month period preceding the redundancy situation. This resulted in one employee with 15 years' service being made redundant while employees with far less service were retained. The tribunal decided that the strict application of so short a period was arbitrary and had an unreasonable impact on otherwise satisfactory long-service employees. (*Fleming* v *Leyland Vehicles*)

In another case, in which a two-year period was used, no account was taken of the fact that one woman's lengthy absence had been caused by maternity leave. Here, the EAT decided that although the selection criterion was reasonable, it had been implemented unfairly.

The lessons to be drawn from case-law and from the perspective of good management practice are these:

☐ Attendance is best considered as only one of several selection criteria.

☐ It should be considered over a reasonably long time period – 18 months is probably close to the shortest reasonable timespan.

☐ It is advisable to consider the reasons for an unsatisfactory attendance record and to pay most attention to unexplained or unauthorised absences.

☐ Minor differences in what are otherwise fully satisfactory attendance records should not be the cause of redundancy selection, particularly for longer-serving employees. For example, if two good employees with eight years' service have average annual absence rates of six days and five days, it would be unfair to use this difference of one day as the sole or main reason for redundancy selection.

Health

This factor is often linked to attendance – with a history of lengthy or frequent sickness absence (though genuine) influencing a redundancy selection. It might, however, go beyond this, with attention paid to health or fitness factors that may not have caused unusually high absence rates but that might be thought to affect future work performance. Cases in which tribunals or the EAT have decided that it was fair to consider health factors have included redundancy selections due to a heart condition, a tendency to gastric ulcers, and mental illness.

Although selection on such a basis may possibly be fair, there is one very important point that needs careful consideration before this can safely be assumed. This is that if selection for a redundancy dismissal is justified primarily on health grounds, it comes very close to equating to a 'normal' ill-health dismissal – ie one in which ill health is the only reason. In consequence, tribunals will expect to see similar care exercised and, in particular, the employee being given adequate opportunity for discussion, explanation, and consideration for other jobs in which the particular health factor would not be so significant an issue. An additional risk derives from disability discrimination law. If an employee could establish that his or her illness met the statutory definition of a disability, then a selection for redundancy on grounds of ill health would amount to a dismissal for having this disability – and this would constitute an unlawful discriminatory act.

As a general rule, therefore, it is inadvisable to use health as the sole or even main criterion, except in cases in which the health record or prognosis is so poor as to indicate the probability of soon having to consider a normal ill-health retirement or dismissal.

Part-timers

At one time it was quite common for employers to use part-time working as a selection criterion. It was argued (without hard evidence) that part-timers were often less committed to their work than full-timers, and that few were their families' principal bread-winners. Making part-timers redundant therefore helped to save the jobs of employees for whom full-time work was a serious necessity.

However, action of this kind could often be shown to constitute indirect discrimination against women, who form a larger proportion of the part-time workforce than men. Later EU and UK legislation made it clear that part-time employees – regardless of gender – should be accorded the same treatment in every aspect of employment as full-timers. Selecting part-time rather than full-time employees for redundancy is no longer an acceptable option.

Multiple criteria

In many instances, employers consider several factors when selecting for redundancy, and this approach has been given support by the tribunals and courts – subject to certain conditions. From a general employment viewpoint, the use of multiple criteria can be advantageous to both employer and employees. For management, it is a more flexible approach that avoids the sometimes unfortunate effect of a single factor producing candidates for redundancy whom the organisation really needs to retain. For employees, it provides the possibility of one adverse factor being outweighed by other more favourable aspects. Against these advantages is the risk of confusion or ambiguity about the weighting given to each criterion, and allegations that the net result of assessments of several factors may be biased in individual cases to produce the result that management wants.

The number and nature of criteria can vary, but the use of three or four, of which length of service is one, is probably the most common practice. Some typical sets of criteria are:

☐ service, competence, attendance

☐ productivity, co-operativeness, service

☐ qualifications, experience, service

☐ skills; age above, at, or close to normal retiring age; attendance; disciplinary record.

The selection of a set of criteria relevant to the particular workforce or type of work is not enough by itself to ensure fairness. Some definition is then required of the relative importance or weighting to be given to each factor and how employees are to be assessed or rated. Unless only one or two employees are involved, the best method is probably to use rating scales. Each employee is then scored for each factor – say, marks out of ten; but if one factor is considered more important than others, it can carry a higher total score. This method is very similar to factor-rated job evaluation or merit rating.

The final step is to ensure that the rating scales are applied consistently and fairly – a particularly important point in large-scale redundancies, when a number of managers may be involved in the assessment and selection process. In one tribunal case, for example, the factors, weights and rating system were all held to be fair, but their application to one employee was not. He was scored at only 50 per cent for attendance, despite having an excellent record, and the tribunal decided that the criteria and scoring method had not been consistently applied.

In summary, the fair and effective use of multiple criteria requires:

☐ criteria relevant to the particular redundancy situation

☐ if appropriate, a weighting of the criteria to reflect their varying importance relative to the needs of the business

- □ a systematic method of rating employees against the criteria
- □ consistency and objectivity in the application of the rating system
- □ records of the assessments and ratings to be made, so that if the results are challenged, fairness and objectivity can be demonstrated.

Indirectly discriminatory criteria

Reference has already been made to the possibility that the selection of part-timers might constitute indirect sex discrimination. Although this is one of the more obvious examples of how discrimination might occur, it is advisable to consider this possibility whatever criteria are to be used. For example, the LIFO method could be discriminatory in an organisation that had only recently begun to recruit women in any numbers. Women might then be disproportionately represented among the short-service staff selected for redundancy. So the effect of any criterion needs to be checked to ensure that, however unwittingly, it would not comparatively disadvantage one particular group covered by anti-discrimination legislation, noting this includes sex, marital status, race, ethnic origin, and disability.

Employees' remedies for breaches of the law

The legal remedies open to trade unions for failures to consult are dealt with in Chapter 7. Here, we consider the action an individual employee may take if that employee considers he or she has been unfairly selected for redundancy. (Claims for redundancy payments are discussed in Chapter 9.)

A complaint that an employee has been unfairly or unreasonably selected for redundancy is, in effect, a complaint of unfair dismissal and is therefore subject to general unfair dismissal legislation, not to any special redundancy provisions.

When a case of alleged unfair selection for redundancy (ie unfair redundancy dismissal) is taken to a tribunal, there is a sequence of issues to be decided:

- □ The first question is whether the employer accepts that there has been a dismissal. If there is disagreement on this point, it is for the employee to produce evidence that a dismissal has occurred.

☐ Next, does the employer accept that the reason was redundancy? If so, the employee needs to show:
  – that the redundancy situation applied to at least one other person
  – that that other person or persons was or were not made redundant.

☐ If redundancy is not accepted as the reason, it is for the employer to produce evidence to show what the reason was (eg the employer may argue the reason was misconduct).

☐ If redundancy is accepted, and regardless of the employee's evidence about other employees, the tribunal will still need to be satisfied that the employer acted reasonably in effecting the dismissal.

If a tribunal finds that an employee's complaint has been established and the redundancy dismissal was indeed unfair, there are three possible remedies it may apply:

☐ *an order for reinstatement* – ie restoring the employee to the same situation as if he or she had not been dismissed, in the same job with full continuity of service and service-related benefits. Although an option, it is unlikely that this would be practicable in most redundancy situations.

☐ *an order for re-engagement* – not necessarily to the same job, and on a date and terms that the tribunal can specify. This is a more likely remedy if there is evidence, for example, that potentially suitable vacancies exist in alternative work.

☐ *compensation* – the most frequently applied remedy. Redundant employees are, of course, entitled in any event to statutory redundancy payments. If they win a case of unfair redundancy dismissal they cannot, however, obtain double payment. Any money the employer has paid them (either the statutory sum or a larger figure derived from the organisation's own redundancy scheme) will be deducted from whatever unfair dismissal compensation the tribunal may award. In many cases, however, the unfair dismissal compensation is likely to exceed the statutory redundancy payment, so there is still a financial incentive for the employee to pursue a case, even though redundancy compensation has been paid.

It is important for an employer defending a complaint of unfair redundancy selection to be able to produce adequate evidence – preferably documented – to show:

☐ whether or not there was any agreed or defined procedure

☐ what criteria were used, and their relevance to the situation and to the needs of the organisation

☐ how the criteria were used, both generally and in relation to the employee making the complaint

☐ that consultation took place with the employee (and, if relevant, with the trade unions)

☐ what consideration was given to finding alternative work

☐ what payments have been made.

Key points

☐ Redundancy is a potentially fair reason for dismissal.

☐ In any disputed case, an employment tribunal will examine whether the redundancy was genuine – *not* whether it was wise.

☐ A redundancy dismissal is automatically unfair if the circumstances of the redundancy apply to one or more other employees who are not dismissed, and if the selection criteria are contrary to any agreed procedure or customary practice.

☐ Redundancy dismissals are also unfair if the reason for selection is related to union membership (or non-membership) or participation in union activities.

☐ There are exceptions to the general principle of trade union criteria being unfair. Redundancy selection may be fair if employees taking industrial action are selected or those whose union activities are in breach of agreed trade union facility arrangements.

☐ The pool of employees from which redundancy dismissals are to be made should include at least all those in jobs that the potentially redundant employees could normally be required to perform.

☐ There is no legal requirement to have an agreed procedure or to apply a standard selection system. In the absence of such agreements or procedures, selection criteria can be determined to fit each redundancy situation – provided the criteria and their application are fair and reasonable.

☐ A redundancy dismissal may be held to be unreasonable if criteria have been applied subjectively or if the actual dismissal process has been mishandled (eg by not providing the opportunity for consultation).

☐ LIFO – although used less widely or exclusively than in the past – remains the criterion least subject to bias and has strong support from case-law as being fair and reasonable. Its disadvantage for the employer is that it makes no distinction between valued and less valued employees.

☐ There is no legal requirement to use LIFO, particularly if other relevant and objective criteria are defined.

☐ Age is an unsatisfactory criterion, except when limited to employees at or near retiring age.

☐ Competence (skill, knowledge, experience, productivity) is probably the most generally satisfactory criterion from an employer's viewpoint. It is accepted by case-law as a fair criterion, provided it is defined and assessed objectively.

☐ Conduct may be a fair criterion (eg selection of those on final warnings), but it is generally best to keep redundancy and disciplinary matters completely separate.

☐ Attitude (co-operativeness, commitment) may be a fair criterion, but there are difficulties in demonstrating objective definition and assessment. If used, this criterion requires great care and the demonstration of examples of the behaviour or incidents that lie behind any assessment.

☐ Attendance (absence rates) is a potentially fair criterion, although generally only in combination with other factors. Attendance records should also be considered over a fairly long timescale (18 months or more).

☐ Health dismissals or retirements are best handled separately from redundancy, except where such terminations are imminent.

☐ To select part-timers for redundancy is unacceptable.

☐ Multiple criteria – a combination of several selection factors – are in many instances the most satisfactory method of redundancy selection. To be used fairly, it generally requires the various factors to be weighted to reflect their relative importance, and employees to be rated or scored for each factor.

☐ Criteria that breach discrimination legislation include marital status and pregnancy. The selection of employees with disabilities could also be a breach of disability legislation.

☐ Employees who consider they have been unfairly selected for redundancy can pursue their complaints under general unfair dismissal legislation – provided they meet certain preconditions.

☐ In a tribunal case, the employee needs to show that the redundancy situation applied to other employees who were not selected; the employer needs to show what the selection criteria were and that they were reasonably applied.

☐ Employees' remedies for unfair redundancy dismissal are reinstatement (likely to be impractical), re-engagement or (more usually) compensation. Monies already paid in redundancy compensation are deductible from the unfair dismissal compensation.

7 MANAGING COLLECTIVE REDUNDANCIES

Although even a single redundancy can have an impact on other employees' attitudes and perceptions and may be the cause of a collective dispute if the workforce considers it unfair, it is in the management of multiple redundancies that employers need to exercise the widest range of industrial relations skills and actions. Partly this is for the obvious reason that when numbers of employees are involved, they will have common interests and concerns that need to be dealt with on a collective basis. But additionally there are important aspects of redundancy legislation that apply specifically to multiple redundancies. These relate to notification and consultation.

Reference has already been made to the desirability in a unionised organisation of concluding a redundancy agreement that sets out how redundancies will be processed. Such agreements need to reflect the legal requirements regarding the information to be given to trade unions and employees' representatives, and the timing and nature of consultation. These requirements have been subject to significant change over the years, reflecting the different views of different governments about trade union rights and the degree to which such issues as consultation should be prescribed by law. Developments in EU labour law have also been – and continue to be – a major influence. This chapter deals with the law as it stood early in 1999, although further change seems inevitable following the UK government's consultative papers on consultation rights in collective redundancies and on amendments to the Acquired Rights Directive (the legislation protecting employee rights on the transfer of undertakings).

Two aspects not covered by legislation but important in the context of effective redundancy management are also dealt with in this chapter:

☐ collective employee assistance
☐ the handling of public relations.

Trade unions and elected employee representatives

Throughout the legislation, notification and consultation rights refer to recognised trade unions or elected employee representatives. Recognised trade unions are those an employer is involved with for collective bargaining – broadly, the negotiation of terms and conditions of employment. Legislation under the government's Fairness at Work proposals will introduce statutory recognition procedures, although there may continue to be confusion or disagreement at times as to whether a union has recognised status. Cases of this kind have had to be resolved in the tribunals when a union has claimed the right to redundancy consultation that the employer has refused.

From such cases, the main recognition principles established by the courts are as follows:

☐ Recognition requires mutuality – a common understanding between employer and trade union of the union's collective bargaining role.
☐ This mutual understanding may be express (ie incorporated in a formal recognition agreement) or implied (ie the way the two parties interact provides evidence of a mutual willingness to negotiate).
☐ To establish implied recognition, there must be clear evidence of relevant negotiating behaviour over a reasonable period of time.
☐ Recognition can exist even if collective bargaining is limited in scope.
☐ The mere use by an employer of the pay and conditions negotiated nationally (eg by a National Joint Council) does not

imply that the employer has recognised the unions involved in these national negotiations. There has to be evidence of direct negotiation between the employer and trade union involved in the redundancy situation.

☐ Recognition for one category of employees within an organisation does not give the trade union recognition rights for other categories, even though the union may have members in these other groups.

To avoid misunderstandings and disputes about a union's recognition status, the simplest solution is to conclude written recognition agreements with the relevant trade unions, ensuring that these agreements are specific about the categories of employees to which they apply. If the organisation has some trade unions with which contact falls short of collective bargaining, the nature of such relationships also merits documentation. For example, a clause along the following lines might be included in a letter or other document given to the union:

> The company is willing for the union to assist any of its members at formal disciplinary or grievance hearings, but the company's acceptance of this union function does not constitute recognition of the union for collective bargaining purposes.

There is no statutory bar on an organisation holding redundancy consultations with a trade union that does not meet the legal criteria for recognition. That is a matter for the organisation itself to decide within the context of its wider industrial relations policy and it could well help to achieve a satisfactory outcome to the redundancy situation.

As at early 1999, the law gave a choice to employers. They could notify and consult with either their recognised trade unions or with elected employee representatives. It is difficult, however, to envisage as satisfactory a situation in which an employer ignores a recognised trade union and chooses instead to deal with a probably *ad hoc* group of employees who may have been elected at very short notice and only because redundancies are looming. Good industrial relations practice indicates that the sensible course of action in a unionised environment would always be to involve the trade unions. It might then be useful for some additional representatives to be elected from among those employees due to be affected by the redundancies, but this could be done under the aegis of the trade union. New legislation is likely to require employers to involve their recognised trade unions where these exist, with the use of separate employee representatives only as an alternative arrangement if, for some reason, trade-union involvement fails.

The position is different if there are no recognised trade unions, and at one time there was no statutory requirement to enter into any form of collective consultation. To comply with an EU directive, it became necessary for the UK to make provision for consulting employees in any collective-redundancy situation, regardless of the existence of a recognised trade union, and the law was amended to require notification and consultation with elected employee representatives. However, there is no statutory requirement on either the employer or employees to initiate elections: whether employees elect representatives is entirely a matter for them. In pre-1999 legislation there was no statutory prescription as to how elections should be conducted, although the new Fairness at Work legislation will set out a formal procedure. If employee representatives are elected, the notification and consultation arrangements are the same as for trade unions. If they are not elected, no form of collective notification or consultation is possible and this element of the law does not apply.

Regardless of the strict legal position, an employer of a non-unionised workforce facing multiple redundancies may find it helpful to suggest that the employees concerned elect some representatives to meet for discussions with the management. There will almost certainly be matters of equal concern to all those involved, and it can be far more effective to recognise this and respond through some form of collective representation than either to ignore the existence of common interests or try to explain the same issues separately to each individual.

Notification

There are two forms of notification required by statute – to the Secretary of State (Department of Trade and Industry – DTI) and to the recognised trade union(s) or elected employee representatives. As at early 1999, the notification to the DTI applied only when an organisation proposed to make 20 or more employees redundant – although this limit is likely to be reduced or abolished by pending legislation. The notification (using a standard form, HR1) has to be made not later than:

□ 30 days before the first dismissal takes effect – for 20 to 99 redundancies

□ 90 days before the first dismissal – for 100 or more redundancies.

The form asks for brief details of the organisation, its location and size of workforce, and the numbers and types of jobs likely to be involved in the redundancy, but not the names of the employees concerned. The submission of this form does not bind the organisation to putting these redundancies into effect, and if circumstances change so that fewer (or more) redundancies are required, all that is needed is to inform the DTI of such changes. This DTI notification is due whether or not there are any trade unions or elected employee representatives.

It is a statutory requirement that a copy of form HR1 is given to the trade union(s) or elected employee representatives if they exist, but this does not constitute the full range of information that must be provided to them. The law specifies that notification to the trade union(s) or elected employee representatives must additionally be in writing and state:

□ the numbers and description (not names) of the employees it is proposed to dismiss on grounds of redundancy

□ the total number of employees of that description – in effect, the nature and size of the pool from which selection for redundancy will be made

□ the reasons for the redundancies

□ how and when the redundancies will be effected

□ the proposed selection criteria and procedure

□ the proposed method for calculating redundancy payments – ie whether payments will be restricted to the statutory sums and if not, how any additional payments will be calculated.

It is of considerable importance that these formal notification procedures are followed and, in particular, that full notification is in writing. The date of this written notification is normally taken as the date on which consultation was opened – and in the event of a dispute as to whether or not the organisation has met its legal consultative obligations, the existence of a copy of this written notification may be vital evidence. In practice, the issue of the written notification can be linked to the opening of face-to-face consultation, as described in the next section.

Consultation

If some form of collective employee representation already exists – either through a recognised trade union or a staff association or joint consultative committee – it is a matter of sound industrial relations, regardless of the law, to use this for discussions about impending redundancies. But unless these discussions meet the statutory provisions regarding collective redundancy consultation, an employer can suffer expensive legal penalties. There have been cases in which otherwise well-intentioned employers have initiated discussions with their trade unions but have failed to comply with the legal timescale and consequently had to pay large 'protective awards' (described later in this chapter) to the employees concerned.

Employers often have difficulty matching the detailed notification requirements with the need to begin consultation at the earliest opportunity. They may have developed firm proposals which it is evident will lead to some redundancies, but cannot be specific about the actual number until more analytical work is done or until more is known about the effect of various redundancy avoidance measures. Regarding the selection methods, they may also take the very sensible line that this is something they wish to evolve in discussion with the trade unions rather than announce in advance. Although all these reasons are sound from a common-sense or good-practice viewpoint, they are not a defence against a failure to meet the statutory requirements, as an EAT case illustrates:

> An engineering company notified a recognised trade union of impending redundancies but was not specific about the details. Thus, in relation to the proposed method of selection for redundancy, the company told the union that 'this would be determined in consultation with union representatives'. The union brought a case (also involving a dispute about timescales) that

included an allegation of a failure to comply with the statutory criteria. The company argued that it was a matter of good industrial relations to leave the details open for discussion with the union. The EAT rejected this defence. The gist of the EAT ruling was that effective consultation cannot take place until the trade union has received details of how the employer proposes to proceed – but that these details can be treated as no more than provisional. They may well have to be altered – not least, as a result of consultation – but the employer does need to indicate a proposed number of redundancies and the proposed method of selection for redundancy. (*E Green & Sons Casting* v *ASTMS*)

A sound way of proceeding, which links the notification and consultation requirements, is to adopt a two-stage approach:

☐ Firstly (although not required by the legislation), it is as well to speak to the relevant trade union representatives or officials on an informal basis and explain why it has become necessary to provide them formally with a notification of possible redundancies. An initial personal contact is nearly always preferable to the first indication being a letter cast in the rather formal terms required by the statute.

☐ At the end of this first meeting (or immediately thereafter) the union can be handed or posted the formal letter of notification. This may need to emphasise the provisional nature of the detailed information it contains. Here is an example of such a letter:

> We are writing, in accordance with the statutory notification and consultation requirements, to confirm the information we gave you at our meeting this morning. Owing to the company's failure to win the XYZ contract, we regret that it will be necessary to reduce the size of the workforce at our ABC plant by the proposed redundancies of 20 fitters and 35 assembly workers. The numbers in these two job categories currently employed are 78 fitters and 125 assembly workers.
>
> The company proposes that the method of selection for redundancy shall be by reference to each employee's competency rating as agreed in the last appraisal reviews.
>
> It is proposed to begin to effect the workforce reduction by . . . (*date*) . . . and to complete it by . . . (*date*) . . . To help in restricting the number of enforced redundancy dismissals

to a minimum, it is proposed to stop all recruitment and overtime working with effect from . . . (*date*), and to invite all employees in the affected job categories to indicate their interest in the possibility of volunteering for redundancy. We are also proposing to waive the statutory limit on a week's pay in the calculation of redundancy payments.

In issuing this notification, the company wishes to stress that the details it contains are our best current, but provisional, estimates. We are very ready to consider and discuss any representations or suggestions you may wish to make and to amend our proposals accordingly should this prove practicable in the light of the difficult commercial circumstances that now obtain.

A copy of form HR1 is attached.

The most common cause of failure to meet the statutory consultation requirements is to assume that the 30- and 90-day periods set out for notification of redundancies to the DTI are sufficient for consultative purposes. What must be recognised is that these are *minimum* periods – the *latest* dates by which consultation must begin. It is worth summarising the consultation requirements:

> An employer who is proposing to dismiss employees on grounds of redundancy must begin collective consultations 'in good time' and in any event, not later than the 30 or 90 days in advance of the first expected dismissal required for statutory notification.

There is no statutory definition of the somewhat vague phrase 'in good time', but there are indications in case-law as to how this is best interpreted. This needs to be linked to consideration of how the tribunals and courts have interpreted the other phrase – 'proposing to dismiss'. However, it is not possible to provide a wholly definitive explanation of these two phrases, partly because they can only be assessed in the light of the specific facts of any disputed case, but also because there is a difference of phraseology between EU and UK law which is as yet unresolved. The relevant EU Directive states that consultations should begin 'when an employer is contemplating collective redundancies', which may seem to suggest a somewhat earlier start than the UK's 'proposing to dismiss'. Be that as it may, the current UK position is probably best taken as that set out by the EAT in a 1991 case:

Matters should have reached a stage where a specific proposal has been formulated and this is at a later stage than the diagnosis of a problem and the appreciation that at least one way of dealing with it would be by declaring redundancies. (*Hough* v *Leyland DAF*)

Both for legal reasons and in terms of good practice, it is highly inadvisable to run risks over the timing of the start of collective consultations. Unless there are very powerful reasons for not doing so, it is best to inform and involve the trade unions as soon as plans are formulated that have redundancy implications. Attempts to conceal such plans (perhaps until they are more fully worked out) are often unsuccessful. Leaks and rumours then sweep through the workforce, damaging morale and placing management on the defensive. Moreover, redundancy rumours are often worse than the reality, so the damage done by delaying consultation may be worse than the reaction to the truth.

The conduct of consultation

Redundancy legislation does not merely require consultation to take place. It specifies some aspects of the process itself, in particular:

☐ Consultation should include consideration of ways of avoiding or minimising the proposed redundancies.

☐ The consultation must be conducted 'with a view to reaching agreement'.

☐ Representations by the trade unions or employee representatives must be given consideration and replied to, with reasons being given if they cannot be accepted.

This set of provisions emphasises the need for consultation to be genuine – which implies that managers must keep an open mind about their original redundancy proposals and be prepared to make changes if the trade unions or employee representatives put forward practicable alternatives. At a 1998 tribunal, a trade union won a case against a company that had consulted about the processing of the proposed redundancies but not about ways of avoiding these job losses. The tribunal concluded that the company had made an irreversible decision to close a factory before opening consultations, and this was in breach of the requirement to conduct meaningful discussions on redundancy avoidance. The financial penalty was considerable – 90 days' pay for each of the employees concerned.

The requirement to attempt to reach agreement does not mean that action can proceed only if agreement is reached. The process is one of consultation, not negotiation. What the law requires and good industrial relations practice dictates is that both parties should adopt a constructive approach to the discussion of a difficult employment situation and make a genuine attempt to agree a course of action. If such attempts fail – for example, by a disagreement about the number of redundancies – then, from the law's perspective, the employer is free to implement whatever action is considered necessary.

There can be very few cases involving a unionised organisation in which full and frank discussions with the trade unions are not both desirable and necessary. Although it may be true that at the end of the day the employer may have to effect redundancies to which a union objects, potential union objections can almost always be modified by providing full reasons for proposed action and by being willing to take the union's views and suggestions into account before final decisions are made. In addition, it should be kept in mind that union representatives have the difficult task of relaying information about the organisation's position to its members. They cannot be expected to do this satisfactorily unless they are given all the facts, with a full explanation not just of the employer's proposals but also of the reasons lying behind these plans.

Another practical point not prescribed in the statute is that all the consultations should be documented, either in the form of minutes of meetings, or by written confirmation in letters to the union of the issues discussed and the outcomes of those discussions. In particular, if the union makes specific proposals that cannot be accepted, the receipt and consideration of these proposals should be acknowledged in writing, together with a clear and adequate explanation why the organisation is not able to accept them. Documentation of this kind may sometimes seem unduly formal, but it can prevent misunderstandings and be vital evidence for the employer if, for any reason, the trade union makes a formal complaint to a tribunal.

There may sometimes be circumstances that make it impracticable to consult as early or as fully as the law normally requires. For example, there might be a sudden and unpredicted collapse of the business's principal customer, the unexpected refusal of a bank or government loan, or a major fire or other disaster. The statute recognises that 'special circumstances' (which are not defined) may arise to prevent normal and timely consultation. In such cases the requirement is to take such steps regarding trade union consultation 'as are reasonably practicable'. Case-law indicates, however, that the following reasons are *unlikely* to be accepted by the courts as justification for failing to comply with the standard consultation provisions:

☐ insolvency due to a gradual deterioration in the business (as distinct from a sudden and unpredictable collapse)

☐ a takeover in which there has been time for an assessment to be made of the employment implications

☐ fear that the news of pending redundancies may cause industrial unrest

☐ fear that news about the redundancies may cause commercial damage.

There are three final points of detail:

☐ Collective consultation is not an alternative to the consultation with individuals described in Chapter 5. Once collective consultation has been concluded and the final decisions taken about the number and type of proposed redundancies, each employee identified for redundancy should be seen as an individual and his or her position discussed with him or her. Failure to consult individually, even when there has been extensive and proper collective consultation, can result in a finding of unfair redundancy dismissal.

☐ There is a requirement to inform and consult with a trade union even if the employees at risk of redundancy are not union members – provided they are in an employee category for which the union has recognition rights.

☐ Although the designated minimum time limits of 30 or 90 days apply only to specified numbers of proposed redundancies, the statute states that 'an employer proposing to dismiss

as redundant *an employee* . . . shall consult . . . etc'. This
implies that trade unions or employee representatives should
be informed and consulted even if there is only one redundancy. This statutory requirement is often overlooked,
although it is a matter of good industrial relations practice,
regardless of the statute, to keep a recognised trade union
informed of all redundancies among the employees it represents.

Remedies for breaches

Complaints about breaches of the statutory consultation provisions can be taken to the employment tribunals only by trade
unions and elected employee representatives – *not* by individual employees, although the effect of the statutory remedy can
be to provide individual employees with awards of additional
pay. If a trade union considers the employer has failed to meet
any of the legal requirements (eg timing, information, nature of
consultation) it can lay a complaint with a tribunal. It may do
so before or after the redundancies have been effected, although
if the complaint is made afterwards, it must be within three
months of the date of the redundancy dismissal about which the
complaint is made. Tribunals have the authority to extend this
three-month time limit if they consider the union could not reasonably have presented the complaint earlier.

There are two actions for a tribunal to take if it finds that an
employer has been in breach of the statute:

☐ It must make a formal declaration to that effect. A declaration is simply a written statement by the tribunal that, in
regard to specified matters, the employer did not comply with
the provisions of the statute. A declaration by itself carries no
financial or other legal penalty. In practical terms, however, a
declaration of this kind may clearly be disadvantageous to the
employer in its future relationship with the trade union, and
may be an embarrassment in a public relations context.

☐ It may make a 'protective award'. This is an award of pay to
the employees for whom consultation was legally faulty for as
long a period as the tribunal thinks fit, subject to the following maxima:

- 28 days, if fewer than 20 employees are involved
- 30 days, for between 20 and 99 employees at one establishment
- 90 days, for 100 or more employees at one establishment.

Protective award payments may be made either to employees (if the complaint is heard before redundancy dismissals occur) or to ex-employees if the tribunal hearing is after the redundancies have taken place. Payments are calculated as full- or part-weeks' pay for whatever period the tribunal considers appropriate. A week's pay is calculated in the same way as for statutory redundancy payments.

Whether a protective award is made (and, if so, for what period) is a matter for the tribunal to decide 'having regard to the seriousness of the employer's default', as the statute puts it. Case-law indicates that the size of the award is not to be decided by a calculation of what employees may have lost in wages, but is more in the form of compensation for a failure to consult. In a leading case the EAT pointed out that the purpose of consultation was to provide time for consideration to be given to ideas for avoiding redundancy. A protective award, said the EAT, is some compensation for the loss of this opportunity to explore alternatives; it is not specifically to cover any loss of remuneration.

There are a number of factors that may lead a tribunal to reduce the size of a protective award or even to make no award at all, despite making a declaration that the employer has been in breach of the consultation provisions. These include:

☐ evidence that, although consultation was inadequate, the employer did make a reasonable attempt to find alternative work or otherwise limit the impact of redundancy

☐ evidence that the trade union was in full possession of the facts, perhaps through some parallel consultative or negotiating processes

☐ the fact that full information had been given to the trade union, but verbally, rather than in writing.

Although a well-intentioned employer may possibly be able to avoid a protective award by showing that the statutory breach was largely technical – rather than a deliberate attempt to avoid consultation – the financial and other risks of losing a case are far too great to justify the adoption of an informal or casual approach to consultation. The only secure protection is to ensure that the whole consultation process – timing, the information provided, and the nature of consultation itself – complies with the detailed provisions described in this chapter. For the organisation with an agreed joint consultative process and a standing redundancy agreement with its recognised trade unions, this is not a difficult matter. The danger arises when insufficient thought or preparation has been given before a redundancy situation occurs as to how it must be managed, with the result that managers evolve procedures on an *ad hoc* basis while a situation is developing.

Collective employee assistance

Measures to assist individual employees, such as outplacement counselling, are dealt with in Chapter 11. The subject here is the action an organisation may take to help ease the impact of large-scale redundancies. This is not to imply that it is impossible to provide individual assistance if large numbers are involved, but rather to examine the additional problems and possibilities that arise in a multiple redundancy situation. The particular measures discussed here are:

☐ pre-redundancy courses
☐ using job centres and other employment agencies
☐ in-house job shops
☐ contacts with potential employers.

Pre-redundancy courses

Although each employee to be made redundant will have his or her own problems and personal circumstances, there is always a core of information and advice relevant to all. One way of assisting these employees is to organise a course to be run during working hours and in the period immediately before the redundancy notices take effect. The approach, and some of the content, can be very similar to a pre-retirement course – of which many organisations have practical experience. In most cases, the topics to include in a pre-redundancy course are:

- an explanation of the redundancy payments and other assistance the organisation may be providing
- the taxable status of redundancy and other termination benefits
- for those eligible, an explanation of early-retirement and pension benefits
- eligibility for, and how to claim, social security benefits
- advice about the management of debt, including mortgage repayments
- information about the options for the investment of redundancy lump sums
- information about employment and training schemes
- advice about making job applications and being interviewed
- advice about sources of further information.

It is essential that information and advice about these issues is accurate and authoritative, and it may well be that the organisation's own staff is not sufficiently expert to cover all the topics. Assistance can then be sought from relevant external sources – such as a building society speaker to talk about the mortgage repayment issue, a representative from the area Training and Enterprise Council (TEC) to provide information about training schemes, and a qualified and independent financial adviser to outline and comment on the investment of lump sums. This last point needs treating with particular care, because it is an offence for a non-qualified or non-certified person to provide investment advice.

Using job centres and employment agencies

Rather than leaving it to each employee to contact the local job centre or employment agencies, the organisation itself can – with the employees' agreement – approach these bodies and provide details of the skills and experience coming onto the job market as a result of the redundancies. This should not prevent individual staff from pursuing their own enquiries, but many redundant employees can be assisted by their employer circulating a well-prepared and professionally presented résumé of their job history to local employment organisations.

A large-scale example is provided by British Coal, which had
to manage an extremely large reduction in its national workforce over a period of many years. British Coal developed a computerised database of its redundant employees and was very
active in publicising the availability of the skills of this surplus
workforce throughout the coal-mining areas. It was able to
match requirements submitted by employers, job centres and
other employment agencies against this database to produce
names of suitable candidates. Few organisations are large
enough or have sufficiently long-running redundancy programmes to operate to this degree of sophistication, but the
practice of contacting employment agencies with details of the
employees concerned is of general application.

In-house job shops

Some organisations have found it helpful to set up a temporary employment office or job shop on their own premises
during a major run-down. Job centres can sometimes provide
personnel to staff a facility of this kind and may be able to link
it to the computerised job database to which the centres are
networked. Alternatively, the organisation's own personnel
department staff may run the facility, obtaining details of
vacancies from the local job centre and directly from other
employers, or the job shop may be operated by an outplacement consultant.

Contacts with other employers

Whether or not a job shop is provided, the organisation can take
positive steps to contact other employers who may have a potential interest in recruiting from among the redundant staff. Most
organisations have extensive knowledge of other employers –
not necessarily local – who employ staff with similar skills, and
direct contacts with them may prove of as much, if not more,
value than approaching employment agencies. Many jobs are
filled normally without advertising and without the use of job
centres and agencies. Companies may rely on speculative applications or draw recruits from waiting lists of enquirers. By contacting such employers direct, the organisation with surplus

staff may be able to find jobs that will never be registered with the agencies or advertised.

Contacts with other employers may also use informal networks, the first approach being, perhaps, a telephone call from the personnel manager of the organisation declaring redundancies to the personally known personnel manager of another organisation operating in the same field. This can be followed up by sending well-prepared CVs of redundant staff, provided care is taken to preserve confidentiality of personal details unless express permission is given by the persons concerned for these details to be released.

Redundancy and public relations

In many locations, companies and other employing organisations are very much part of their local communities and their activities attract considerable public interest. Local and regional media (press, radio and TV) often feature their local employers' successes and failures, redundancies on any scale always being a potential news item. In good times, one of the most powerful aids to recruitment is a reputation as a good employer; how redundancies are handled can contribute significantly to this reputation. Even an internally well-managed redundancy programme can fail in this respect if the organisation ignores the public interest and refuses co-operation with the media.

It is often better, therefore, to take the initiative and inform the media about impending redundancies as soon as this information has been released to the unions and employees. They, of course, should be told first: for employees to hear about possible redundancies for the first time by reading the local paper is a disastrous start to any redundancy process. It should be recognised, though, that as soon as employees are told, someone is likely to tell a local reporter, who will then want to file a story as quickly as possible in order to beat the competition. If the organisation does not take steps to ensure the media are informed accurately and promptly about what is happening (and why) there is a real risk of distorted press (or other media) reports. The standard method for releasing information is the short, simply written press release, drafted in lay language, and sent simultaneously to all relevant media outlets. It should provide the name and telephone number of a person to contact for more information, and this person must be fully briefed in order to deal with whatever questions are likely to be asked.

Another situation in which managers need public relations skills occurs when takeovers or mergers are announced. This often generates intense media speculation about the possible effect on jobs. Managers being interviewed about such developments and wanting to talk about business strategy and commercial rationale are then pressed instead by media to say how many employees will lose their jobs. In replying, managers need to consider the impact of what they say, both on the workforce at large and on the trade unions – particularly if unions have not yet been brought into the picture. A reply by a senior manager in a TV interview to a question about job losses that might result from the merger of two large manufacturing companies, illustrates a sensible way of dealing with this type of enquiry. Asked 'How many employees are likely to be made redundant?', he replies 'We shall be discussing the employment situation with our trade unions, and we shall make sure our employees are the first to be told about the outcome.' Managers should certainly avoid being drawn into speculating publicly about possible redundancies.

However, it may not be possible to prevent such speculation by the media. Stories may appear in the local or national press that a merger (or some other business development) is likely to lead to a specified and large number of job losses. If the actual number is known by the company or companies concerned, they should by that time have notified the trade unions or employee representatives, so public confirmation or correction of the media story should not cause problems. But if the employment implications have not yet been fully worked out, that is what should be said – not a blanket rebuttal, which might be taken as implying that no redundancies will occur.

Two case-studies

The two case-studies below illustrate how a number of the measures described earlier in this chapter have been put into practice by organisations faced with the management of large-scale redundancies.

British Shoe Corporation

In this example, the emphasis of the company's approach was on help-ing displaced staff find employment elsewhere. Selection for redun-dancy was not an issue, because the whole workforce was disbanded. The British Shoe Corporation, part of the Sears retail group, had a turnover of £450 million and 11,000 employees. In late 1997, Sears decided to break up the shoe business and find buyers for its various subsidiaries such as Dolcis and Roland Cartier. As a result of these sales, 7,000 staff were offered employment with the new owners, but 3,500 retail employees and 350 head-office staff faced redundancy. The company accepted responsibility for helping these displaced staff find other employment and put together a project team of HR specialists and line managers to plan and operate an outplacement programme. External assistance was bought in to train the team in coaching and career management skills. It was decided that the programme needed a high-profile, physical focal point, so a career support centre was opened in the company's main location.

Open from 9am to 6pm and operating on a drop-in basis, the centre provided a wide range of resources for staff embarking on job searches, including trade publications and directories, Internet access and a com-puter notice-board with details of job vacancies drawn from a national database of major retailers. All employees were also invited to a two-day job-search workshop which gave advice on such topics as CV-production and interview preparation. Specialist counselling was on offer and com-puterised, and NVQ-accredited training packages were made available for staff needing to learn new IT skills to improve their employability.

Once actual redundancies had to be declared, a job-support pack was sent to the home of each employee involved, together with a fortnightly bulletin of around 1,500 vacancies in other organisations, collated from contacts, trade publications and other sources. An out-placement consultancy was used to contact some 400 other com-panies for the details of possible job opportunities. Redundant employees were also able to contact a dedicated telephone helpline for advice on any aspect of job search. Staff who needed to be retained until the end of the programme were paid retention bonuses. As a result of the whole programme, the company was able to achieve a near-100 per cent success rate in helping its redundant staff find alternative jobs.

Case-study

IBM (UK)

In this (earlier) example, in addition to assistance with job search the company offered staff significant financial assistance to volunteer for redundancy. Selection for redundancy was an important aspect, because a large part of the workforce was due to be retained.

In 1990, IBM (UK) found it necessary to effect a reduction of over 2,000 staff from its 10,500 workforce. The company had a policy of avoiding enforced redundancies but was not able to use natural wastage effectively, owing to very low staff turnover. A scheme was therefore launched to attract volunteers, targeted to achieve specific changes in the company's age and skills profiles. The incentives to volunteer for redundancy were:

☐ lump sums of two months' salary per year of service, up to a maximum of 24 months.

☐ an immediate pension for staff aged 50 and above

☐ for staff aged between 40 and 55, enhancements to pension entitlements made by paying age-related lump sums of from 2 to 12 months' pay to purchase additional pension benefits

☐ an option to purchase company cars at a favourable price

☐ participation in a register for freelance work.

Outplacement counselling was also on offer to staff accepted for redundancy. Volunteers who could not be accepted were also given explanations and counselling. The scheme was first opened to the older HQ employees, from whom the most reductions were sought. The scheme was then extended to other employee categories on a staged basis until the full target of job-cuts had been achieved. The scheme attracted 2,300 volunteers, fully meeting all the company's targets without the need for compulsory redundancies. The company estimated that the costs involved would be recovered in less than two years through saving the salaries and on-costs of the staff who left.

The specific circumstances and organisational objectives in these two cases were unique to the companies concerned, and their staff reduction programmes should not be taken as models just to be copied. They demonstrate, however, several common points of principle with broad applicability to most cases of multiple redundancies:

☐ The details of a redundancy management programme should be designed to fit the particular circumstances and business needs of each case. So the priority given to various measures will vary from case to case.

☐ In anything other than the complete closure of an organisation on one date, there is a need for careful selectivity in the use of a scheme to attract volunteers.

☐ For older employees, their pension position is often the most important single issue.

☐ Intensive, comprehensive and continuous employee information and consultation is needed.

☐ Employees need and appreciate a wide range of measures to help them cope with redundancy and prepare for successful job search.

Key points

☐ Some types of practical action which employers may take are specific to situations involving multiple, rather than individual, redundancies.

☐ Some legal provisions apply only to situations in which the employees are in categories for which there are recognised trade unions or elected employee representatives.

☐ The legal provisions specific to recognised trade unions apply only to those unions involved in collective bargaining with the employer.

☐ To avoid disputes about unions' recognition status, it is advisable to conclude formal recognition agreements with the selected unions.

☐ Recognised unions have to be consulted before any redundancies take place within the employee categories for which they are recognised, whether or not the employees concerned are union members.

☐ Consultations with unions or elected employee representatives must begin at the earliest opportunity, ie as soon as the organisation has developed proposals expected to result in redundancies.

☐ In any event, consultation must not start later than 30 days before the first redundancy (if 20 to 99 redundancies are expected) or 90 days (for 100 or more redundancies).

☐ Early information and consultation is advisable, regardless of the statutory requirement, to prevent the adverse effects of leaks and rumours.

☐ Consultation to meet statutory requirements has to begin by written notification to the trade unions or employee representatives, specifying the reasons for proposed redundancies, the numbers and types of employees involved, the proposed method of their selection, the timing and method of the proposed dismissals, and the way compensation payments will be calculated.

☐ This information should not be delayed because of the possibility of the details being changed – the requirement is to notify of *proposed* action, not necessarily what will eventually be effected.

☐ In practice, written notification is best preceded by a meeting with the employee or trade union representatives.

☐ The law (and good practice) requires consultation to be real and in good faith – that is, for the employer to consider seriously the union's views and suggestions and be prepared to change the original redundancy proposals. Statutory consultation does not, however, require all issues to be subject to union agreement.

☐ There is a legal requirement to inform the trade unions of the reasons why any union proposal cannot be accepted. For this and other practical reasons, it is good practice to ensure all consultation is documented.

☐ The statute allows the detailed consultation requirements to be set aside if special circumstances arise (such as a sudden and unexpected business collapse or a major fire). But fears of industrial unrest or commercial damage caused by timely consultation are not sufficient reasons for non-compliance.

☐ Trade unions or employee representatives (but not individual employees) can seek legal remedies for an employer's failure to comply with the statutory consultative provisions. The two remedies are a declaration of non-compliance and 'protective awards' of up to 90 days' pay for the employees concerned –

the actual amount being dependent on the tribunal's assessment of the seriousness of the breach and the number of employees involved.

☐ In addition to individual help, measures to assist groups of potentially redundant employees can include:
  – pre-redundancy courses to provide information and advice on all aspects of personal finance and job-search
  – the use of job centres and other employment agencies to find alternative employment
  – setting up in-house job shops, perhaps staffed by external employment specialists
  – contacting other employers and publicising the availability of the displaced employees.

☐ There is a public relations aspect to large-scale redundancies. Organisations are advised to release accurate and timely information to the local media to prevent distorted stories and to project an image as good employers.

☐ Case studies indicate the importance of designing redundancy programmes to meet specific business circumstances and objectives.

☐ Volunteer schemes in particular are best carefully targeted on sectors and age-groups in which leavers would most readily resolve the organisation's workforce surpluses.

☐ Fair selection methods and the sensitive handling of dismissals (and of the rejection of volunteers who cannot be released) are of major importance.

☐ For older employees, pensions are often the most important issue of concern.

☐ Extensive and continuous information and consultation play a major part in reducing the adverse effects of a redundancy programme.

☐ Employees need, and appreciate, the provision of a wide range of assistance in coping with redundancy.

8   LAY-OFFS AND SHORT TIME

Before any of the current employment legislation reached the statute book, it was common for companies experiencing a temporary shortfall in orders to cut their employment costs by laying workers off without pay or by working less than a full week and cutting earnings proportionately. This practice was clearly open to abuse, some firms reducing employees almost to the status of casual workers with little security of job or earnings. Trade union pressure put a stop to many of the more extreme cases, and in time the use of lay-offs and short time came to be seen as having benefits for employees in certain situations. In particular, these measures could be used to save jobs as an acceptable alternative to redundancy dismissals. However, concern about possible abuse still remained, and legislation was consequently introduced within the Redundancy Payments Act 1965 (now incorporated in ERA) to give employees a means of challenging the use of protracted periods of lay-off or short time. Before considering how lay-offs and short-time working can still be used as a helpful and acceptable way of avoiding redundancy, it is necessary to examine four kinds of legal constraint that affect the use of these measures:

- contract law
- statute law relating to constructive dismissal
- the Wages Act 1986 provisions relating to deductions or stoppages of pay
- The provisions in ERA dealing specifically with lay-offs and short time.

Contract law

Under the general principles of contract law it is a breach of contract for the employer not to pay the full agreed salary or wages while the employee is available for and willing to work. During lay-offs or short time, it is a necessary part of the arrangement that employees do maintain their availability to resume normal working when the employer so requires. It follows that to lay off an employee with no wages, or to cut an employee's pay during a period of short-time working, constitutes a fundamental breach of contract – unless the contract makes specific provision for such action. There are three ways in which such contractual provisions may come into existence:

☐ Documents issued to employees describing the terms and conditions of employment may make specific reference to the possible use of lay-offs or short time, stating the circumstances in which these measures may be used and the provisions relating to pay. Provided it is clear that these documents constitute a statement of contractual terms, the organisation can then proceed to use lay-offs and short time – subject to the specific statutory provisions.

☐ In the absence of a previously agreed contractual provision, it is open to the employer to try to obtain employees' individual and formal agreement to a new contractual term, at the time when a period of lay-off or short-time working seems a sensible measure to implement.

☐ In a unionised organisation in which many of the employees' terms and conditions of employment are determined by negotiation with the trade unions, the terms of a collective agreement for the use of lay-offs or short time may be incorporated in individual contracts of employment.

Constructive dismissal

Unfair dismissal legislation has provided employees with a simpler legal remedy for breaches of contract than pursuing claims for such breaches through the courts. This is the concept of constructive dismissal. In brief, a complaint of constructive dismissal can be made to an employment tribunal if an employee leaves because the employer has acted in a way that is, or equates to, a fundamental breach of contract. Stopping or cutting wages, when no contractual provision exists to legitimise such action, is just such a breach – although the employee can rarely bring a constructive dismissal claim while still in employment.

Wages Act 1986

This Act made it unlawful to make deductions from employees' pay, other than those required by statute (eg PAYE) and those the employee has formally agreed in writing. After some legal confusion as to whether the withholding of *all* pay amounted to a deduction, it is now certain that pay stoppages or reductions of the type implicit in lay-offs and short-time working could contravene the provisions of the Wages Act 1986 – unless the pay changes were covered by a contractual provision or other specific agreement. In the absence of such arrangements, employees who were told that short-time working was being introduced with proportionate pay reductions or that they were being laid off with no pay (but not dismissed) could take two courses of action:

□ make a claim to a tribunal under the Wages Act 1986 for an order for recovery of lost wages

□ leave the organisation's employment and make a claim for compensation for constructive dismissal on the grounds that the pay cut or reduction amounted to a fundamental breach of contract. In this case, a tribunal could award the full range of unfair dismissal compensation – not just an amount to cover the unpaid wages.

The employee could not, however, be compensated twice for the same loss.

Lay-off and short-time provisions

The ERA provisions may appear relatively simple in principle but are complex and sometimes ambiguous to apply in practice. They were described by an EAT judge in 1984 as 'the despair of all who have been concerned with the interpretation of industrial legislation since the scheme of statutory entitlement to a redundancy payment was introduced in 1965'.

The essence of the provisions is that employees can apply for standard statutory redundancy payments if lay-offs or periods of short time last longer than a specified period. (This is the one exception to the rule, stressed in previous chapters, that redundancy occurs only when a dismissal takes place. For the purposes of these ERA provisions, no dismissal is necessary before an entitlement to redundancy may accrue.) The apparently simple principle is hedged about with a complex set of definitions and rules:

- Lay-offs are covered only if they meet two criteria:
  - there must be an express contractual provision (ie an unambiguous written statement incorporated in the contract) to cease paying wages if no work can be provided
  - there must be no contractual provision to pay any form of wages during a lay-off, and no wages (however small) must actually be paid.

  However, statutory guarantee payments (described later in this chapter) do not count as wages for this purpose because they are not contractual.
- For short-time working to qualify, the amount of wages paid each week must be less than half the normal week's pay. A week's pay has to be calculated in the same way as for redundancy payments (explained in detail in Chapter 9). As with lay-offs, statutory guarantee payments are discounted, because they are not contractual.
- Before employees can take advantage of the provisions, they must be laid off (or on short time) for either:
  - a period of four consecutive weeks, or
  - a total of six weeks in any period of 13 weeks, with no more than three of the affected weeks being consecutive.

A number of collective agreements about lay-offs and short time provide for small retention payments to be made during lay-offs and for a guaranteed minimum level of earnings of over half a normal week's wage during short time. In these instances, use of the statutory provisions is ruled out. To qualify, there must be no pay during lay-offs and less than half pay during short time.

If an employee in a situation that meets the statutory criteria wishes to bring it to an end by claiming a redundancy payment, there is a very detailed procedure with strict time limits that must be followed:

☐ The employee must give the employer written notice of an intention to claim a redundancy payment.

☐ This notice must be given within four weeks of the last week of lay-off or short time to which the claim refers.

☐ Having received this notice of an intention to claim, the employer may serve a written counter-notice on the employee, stating that liability for a redundancy payment will be contested.

☐ This counter-notice must be served within seven days of receipt of the employee's notice of intention.

☐ If a counter-notice has been issued, the employee can take his or her claim further only by applying to an employment tribunal. If no such application is made, the claim for redundancy falls.

☐ At a tribunal hearing, the only defence the employer is allowed to offer is that at the time the employee submitted the notice of intention, it was reasonable to assume there would be a return to normal full-time working within four weeks.

☐ If the employer does not issue a counter-notice, or withdraws a counter-notice after it has been issued, statutory redundancy compensation becomes payable, provided the employee complies with the following provisions about giving notice.

☐ To obtain a redundancy payment, the employee must give notice of termination – ie must resign. The amount of notice must be either one week or the minimum notice specified in the contract of employment if that is more than a week. There are three different time limits involved:

– If the employer does not serve a counter-notice, the employee must give notice of termination within four weeks of serving the original notice of intention to claim a redundancy payment.

– If the employer withdraws a counter-notice, the employee must give notice within three weeks of the date of withdrawal.

– If the case goes to a tribunal and the employee is awarded redundancy compensation, notice must be given within three weeks of being informed of the tribunal's decision.

There are two other relevant statutory provisions – the exclusion from the provisions just described of lay-offs or short time caused wholly or mainly by strike action; and the requirement to pay statutory 'guarantee payments' to employees in certain circumstances (see below).

Strike and lock-out exclusions

Periods of lay-off or short time wholly or mainly attributable to strikes are excluded from the statutory regulations. An odd feature of this provision is that the strike action causing the lay-off need not be within the organisation in which the laid-off employee works. Indeed, there have been a number of tribunal cases in which employees have claimed, but failed to obtain, redundancy payments when the strikes causing their lay-offs were shown to be in other organisations.

Statutory guarantee payments

The purpose of these payments (another ERA provision) is to provide a guarantee of some pay (albeit at a very modest level) for employees whose earnings are cut through lay-offs or short time. The guarantee can be described as a right to a specified minimum sum for any day in which the employee is not provided with work and consequently loses all or some pay. As with redundancy claims, the rules are complicated:

- ☐ Unlike the redundancy provisions, which are concerned with the number of *weeks* on lay-off or short time, guarantee payments are concerned with 'workless *days*'. There is no minimum period – an entitlement can accrue for just one day with no work and no (or reduced) pay.
- ☐ Entitlement is limited, however, to five days in any rolling period of three months.
- ☐ Any contractual pay for a workless day (such as a negotiated retainer or an organisation's own minimum-earnings guarantee) has to be set off against the current statutory guarantee day rate – a sum normally increased annually by government regulation. In other words, anything paid by the employer is deducted from the statutory entitlement. So if the 'domestic' guarantee is the same or exceeds the statutory figure, no statutory sum is payable.

- Unlike the redundancy provisions, whether or not the employer has a contractual right to stop or cut pay is irrelevant. Claims for the statutory guarantee can be pursued when pay stoppages are in breach of contract, as well as when such stoppages are within the contract of employment.
- To qualify for a guarantee payment, an employee must have been employed continuously for one month – this month ending on the day before the day for which a guarantee payment is claimed.
- Guarantee payments cannot be claimed by employees on performance contracts not expected to last more than three months or by those on fixed-term contracts of three months or less.
- The non-availability of work on a day for which payment is claimed must be due either to a diminution in the work for which the employee is contractually employed or to 'any other occurrence' that affects the normal running of the business. Other occurrences have been held by tribunals and courts to be such events as fires and floods – something other than just a simple internal decision by the employer to slow down the work.
- Three reasons for lay-off are excluded from the guarantee provisions:
  - strikes, lock-outs or other industrial action involving any employee of the business or of any associated businesses
  - an unreasonable refusal by the employee to do suitable alternative work
  - failure by employees to meet a reasonable requirement by the employer to hold themselves available for work.
- Claims for guarantee payments must be made initially to the employer. If the employer refuses to pay, the employee must make an application to an employment tribunal within three months, counting from the day for which payment is being claimed.

It is possible to escape from these complicated regulations by having instead a collective agreement, applying jointly with the recognised trade unions to the Secretary of State for Employment for an exemption order. The criteria for obtaining such an order are as follows:

☐ There must be a collective agreement that provides for guaranteed minimum payments – although there is no requirement that these provisions have to equal or be better than the statutory payments.

☐ The agreement must provide for some form of independent arbitration in the event of a dispute.

☐ The agreement must also give a right to employees to complain to an employment tribunal about a failure to pay.

There are a number of exemption orders in existence – several covering complete industries, because they derive from national collective bargaining in such bodies as the National Joint Council for the Building Industry.

Practical implications

The complex legal provisions concerning lay-offs and short time might appear to constitute powerful reasons for not using these measures. This would, however, be a mistaken view which, if followed generally, would almost certainly result in redundancies having to be effected that at present are being avoided. The motor industry provides a good example. Lay-offs, and particularly periods of short-time working, have several times enabled car manufacturing companies to keep their skilled workforces together during recessionary periods – thus avoiding both redundancies and the costs and risks of trying to reassemble a workforce when order volumes improve. Few if any adverse legal effects have been experienced, because the companies concerned have ensured their schemes are legally sound.

As part of a set of measures to avoid redundancy, there is consequently considerable benefit in the operation of lay-off and short-time schemes – subject to some common-sense criteria:

☐ The over-riding principle is that these schemes should be contractual – either directly or by express incorporation from relevant collective agreements – thus avoiding all the potential statutory pitfalls.

☐ It is preferable for lay-off schemes to provide for some form of guaranteed retention payment, however small, rather than no pay at all.

☐ Agreements about short-time payment should include a

guaranteed minimum. (Most organisations with a guaranteed minimum agreement also pay more than the statutory sum.)

☐ Trade union agreement should be sought for applying for an exemption order from the statutory guarantee regulations, provided the collective agreement meets the statutory criteria.

☐ Periods of lay-off and short time should be kept as short as possible.

☐ Consideration should be given during a protracted period of difficulty to the possibility of breaking periods of lay-off by short spells of full- or short-time working – even if only for a matter of a day or two.

For organisations currently without any contractual provision for lay-offs or short time – as applies generally throughout most of the public sector – the question arises whether they should attempt to introduce new contractual clauses. Organisations that do not expect to undergo significant fluctuations in their work-load may well consider such action unnecessary. But if there are significant uncertainties about future work requirements, or if new commercial pressures may cause large fluctuations in the workload, the introduction of lay-off and short-time provisions may be worth serious consideration.

Because of the importance of the contractual position, the introduction of the relevant new conditions into contracts of employment would have to be handled with care. The essence of a contract (and of a variation to a contract) is that it requires mutual consent. The unilateral imposition of new contractual conditions by the employer is a legally dangerous procedure, open to claims that the existing contract has been broken. There are, though, at least three possible ways of proceeding which would not infringe the principles of contract law:

☐ In a unionised organisation, the changes can be made by concluding a relevant agreement with the trade unions – provided existing individual contracts say that all union agreements are incorporated.

☐ In the absence of this collective mechanism, new contractual clauses providing for lay-offs and short time may be introduced within current employment contracts by agreement with each employee concerned. This is impracticable for a large workforce but could be done within a small organisation. If so, it must be accepted that the result may be that some employees agree and others do not.

☐ The new contractual provisions could be used only for newly appointed staff, no attempt being made to persuade existing employees to agree to contractual variations. This, too, will lead to individuals having to be dealt with differently when the need for lay-offs or short time occurs.

Key points

☐ Lay-offs and short-time working can make an important contribution to the avoidance of redundancy.

☐ There are, however, some complex legal issues involving contract law, dismissal legislation, the Wages Act, and specific ERA regulations.

☐ The overriding requirement is that any use of cuts or reductions to pay should be provided for within the contracts of employment.

☐ Such provision may be either specific or by the incorporation into contracts of the terms of collective agreements.

☐ To use lay-offs or short time without this contractual provision can lead to claims for breach of contract, unfair dismissal or the recovery of lost wages via the Wages Act.

☐ If no pay is provided during lay-offs, and if pay during short time is less than half normal pay, employees may apply for redundancy compensation after a period specified in the legislation.

☐ The employer may counter this claim by arguing that a resumption of normal working is expected within a statutorily specified period.

☐ Employees may also claim statutory guarantee payments for workless days for which no (or reduced) pay was given.

☐ Employers with collective agreements for guaranteed minimum pay may apply, with their trade unions, for an exemption from the statutory guarantee scheme.

☐ To avoid all or most legal complications, employers must have relevant contractual provisions that make some form of guaranteed minimum payment during lay-offs, and guaranteed minima during lay-offs at or above the statutory level.

☐ Organisations currently without a contractual right to use lay-offs or short time might find it helpful to introduce such provisions – provided they do so by consent of individual employees or by collective agreements, if these can be incorporated in employment contracts.

9 REDUNDANCY COMPENSATION

It is as much a moral as a legal view that employees who lose their jobs through no fault of their own should be compensated in some way. Although redundancy does not inevitably result in a period of unemployment with consequent financial problems, for many of those involved there is a period of job-searching and the possibility that a new job, when found, may involve additional travel-to-work time, perhaps lower immediate earnings and (in some cases) the trauma of moving house. In all cases there is the loss of employment continuity, which in many organisations results in new employees being eligible for a lower level of benefits than longer-service staff. The loss of continuity also erodes the new employee's legal rights, because many of these rights (such as the right to redundancy compensation and protection against unfair dismissal) are dependent on accruing a certain length of service. Many employers accept some responsibility for assisting redundant employees at this difficult time, and one aspect of this assistance is the payment of redundancy compensation – the main subject of this chapter. Other forms of assistance are dealt with in Chapter 11.

As with so many aspects of redundancy management, whatever is done regarding compensation needs to incorporate an organisation's own policies and a quite complex set of statutory requirements. The latter also form the minimum baseline, which may be the most an organisation in serious financial difficulties can afford.

The principle that employees who lose their jobs through redundancy should receive financial compensation was first incorporated in legislation in 1965. Redundancy had not been a significant employment issue in the immediate post-war years but, as a result of economic problems in the early 1960s, many companies cut their workforces – sometimes giving the employees concerned no more than basic notice pay. The Redundancy Payments Act 1965 was then introduced, giving all employees who met its eligibility criteria a guarantee of at least a basic level of compensation. Since then, there have been several developments:

☐ With only minor changes, the provisions of the original Act have been incorporated in the ERA.

☐ A scheme under which employers could claim rebates of part of their redundancy payments from government funds has been abolished.

☐ Many employers have decided that the statutory redundancy payments are inadequate and have introduced their own, more liberal, schemes, some of which include additional arrangements for enhancing pensions and providing other termination benefits.

This chapter starts by explaining the statutory provisions and then examines the wider range of compensation arrangements that employers can introduce as a part of their own personnel policies. The statutory provisions are dealt with under six headings:

☐ eligibility
☐ normal retiring age
☐ continuous employment
☐ entitlements
☐ calculating the payments
☐ offsetting pension payments.

Compensation arrangements beyond those required by statute are discussed under two further headings:

☐ non-statutory financial compensation
☐ other forms of compensation.

Eligibility for statutory payments

The first criterion for eligibility for a statutory redundancy payment is that there must have been a dismissal, but not all employees who are dismissed on grounds of redundancy are entitled to a payment. The excluded categories are:

☐ those with less than two years' continuous service

☐ those aged under 20: only continuous service from the age of 18 is counted, so no one under 20 can meet the two-year criterion

☐ those at or above their organisation's normal retiring age, or aged 65 or over if there is no normal retiring age

☐ those not working under genuine contracts of employment (eg self-employed persons)

☐ civil servants and other crown servants, who have separate statutory schemes

☐ domestic servants who are close relatives of their employers

☐ those who ordinarily work outside Great Britain, although if they are made redundant while working temporarily in Great Britain they do acquire compensation rights

☐ employees on fixed-term contracts that include a clause waiving the right to redundancy payments on non-renewal.

National Health Service employees were at one time excluded but were brought within the statutory scheme in 1991. Local authority staff are also within the scheme but have additional statutory entitlements under separate local government regulations.

Normal retiring age

Apart from the definition of 'continuous service', the issue that has caused most legal problems has been the exclusion of employees who are over their normal retiring age. There is no difficulty about this if there is a specific contractual requirement to retire at a defined age, and this has been enforced in practice. Where problems arise is when this fixed age has not been applied consistently and certain groups of staff have been allowed to retire at different ages. There can also be a dispute about the existence of a normal retiring age if retirements are allowed within an age range (say, 60 to 65) but employees claim that in practice most expect to retire at one particular age. If a case reaches a tribunal, it will be resolved by examining the facts along the following lines:

□ Is there a contractual retiring age?

□ If so, has it been adhered to for employees doing broadly the same jobs as the redundant employee? If so, the employee must be under that age to qualify for statutory redundancy pay.

□ If not, and if there is no contractual retiring age, what in practice has been the retiring age of employees in the same position?

□ If the practice has been sufficiently clear to give these employees a reasonable expectation that they will retire at one specific age, that will be taken as the normal retiring age, and redundancy pay cannot be claimed by those above this age.

□ If there is no clear pattern, then the age of 65 will apply as the cut-off for redundancy pay entitlements.

Two general points are worth noting. First, that in the absence of a lower normal retiring age, 65 is used for women as well as men, regardless of the difference in eligibility for the state retirement pension. Secondly, that it is the collective expectation about their normal retiring age of the employees in the same position as the redundant employee that is the test, not the possibly different personal expectations of the individual redundant employee.

Continuous employment

There have been many tribunal cases about redundant employees' length of continuous service. There are two kinds of problems:

□ disagreements about the precise calculation of the two-year period for employees whose unbroken service from appointment to dismissal is very close to the two-year limit

□ disputes as to whether various types of break in service count towards continuous employment.

In assessing the basic two-year requirement or any other service period that future legislation may specify, two dates need to be established – the first and last days of employment. This may seem straightforward, but there are two possible complications:

☐ The first date is not necessarily the first day at work – it is the first day on which the contract of employment comes into force. For example, an employee may accept a contract dated from the first day of the month – say Saturday 1 May. But he or she is not required actually to start work until Tuesday 4 May, after the bank holiday. The two-year qualifying period begins on the 1st, not the 4th.

☐ The end date is not necessarily the last day at work. If no notice has been given (eg by paying in lieu), or the notice has been shorter than the statutory notice entitlement, the last day for continuous employment purposes (termed the 'relevant date') will be the day the statutory notice of one week per year of service up to a maximum of 12 weeks would have expired.

Having defined the start and end date, it can then be seen whether the service meets the two-year criterion, bearing in mind that this is defined as two calendar years of 12 months each – not 104 weeks.

The law deems employment to have been continuous unless the employer can prove otherwise – all the employee has to do is claim continuity. Breaks in employment of less than one full week are disregarded, but a 'week', for this purpose, is one ending on a Saturday. It is therefore possible for a break of longer than seven days not to count as such. For example, a monthly-paid employee resigns and has a last day in employment on Monday 31 August. The job he was going to folds unexpectedly and a re-engagement is agreed with a Thursday 10 September start date. The actual break has been nine days spread across two weeks. But continuity of employment will be maintained because neither of these two weeks is a full week at work ending on a Saturday.

The one-week rule applies to any type of break, except one that follows a redundancy dismissal. If an employee is dismissed on redundancy grounds and is offered and accepts re-engagement (whether or not in the original job), continuity is maintained if employment resumes within four weeks of the dismissal.

Weeks that count as employment include statutory maternity leave and up to 26 weeks during which the employee is unable to work because of sickness or injury. (This applies only when the contract of employment is inoperative during this absence; normally, the contract continues during sickness absence and this maintains continuity.) See also the section on the two-year criterion in Chapter 3, because this explains the way the courts treat various other breaks in employment. The main provision is that continuity of employment is maintained during periods of absence caused by the temporary cessation of work. There is no statutory definition of 'cessation of work', nor is there any defined limit on the length of such periods. If there is a dispute about this, then whether or not a particular period meets the definition is a matter for a tribunal or the courts to decide as a matter of fact, taking account of all the circumstances. Note, however, that a break cannot occur if pay continues during the employee's absence.

Other points that affect assessments of the period of continuous employment are these:

❑ Absence from work through strikes does not break continuity, but the period on strike does not count towards length of service. In other words, an employee with two years' service, one month of which was occupied by strike action, does not have broken service but can count only 1 year 11 months towards the calculation of continuous employment.

❑ For employees who spend some time working abroad (although not to an extent to disqualify them completely), only those weeks of employment count for which National Insurance payments have been made.

❑ If an employee is dismissed or resigns because of sickness and is re-engaged within 26 weeks of the termination, employment is treated as continuous.

Entitlements

The actual sums due under the statutory scheme are based on the redundant employee's age, service and pay – although there are limitations placed on each of these factors. The schedule of payments is:

☐ half a week's pay for each full year of service between the ages of 18 and 22

☐ one week's pay for each full year of service between the ages of 22 and 40

☐ one and a half week's pay for each full year of service from the age of 41 to either normal retiring age or the age of 65 (as explained earlier).

The limitations are:

☐ *age*. Service before 18 and after retiring age is excluded. Between 64 and 65, the total sum due is reduced by one-twelfth for each completed month.

☐ *service*. A maximum of only 20 years can be used in calculating a redundancy payment.

☐ *a week's pay*. There is a ceiling on the amount of a week's pay (£220 in early 1999 – a figure revised annually).

Calculating the payments

To calculate an employee's entitlement, service must be counted from the dismissal date backwards. For example:

An employee is 45 at the time of dismissal and has 12 years' service. The entitlement is:
4 years @ 1½ weeks' pay (service between 41 and 45)
– 6 weeks
8 years @ 1 week's pay (service before 40)   – 8 weeks

Total: 14 weeks' pay

An employee is 53 and has 30 years' service. The entitlement is:
12 years @ 1½ weeks' pay (service from 41 to 53)
– 18 weeks
8 years @ 1 week's pay (maximum available within the 20-year limit)   – 8 weeks

Total: 26 weeks

An employee is 23 and has 7 years' service. The entitlement is:

1 year @ 1 week's pay (service from 22 to 23)

$-$ 1 week

4 years @ $^1\!/_2$ week's pay (service from 18 to 22)

$-$ 2 weeks

Total: 3 weeks' pay

The maximum possible payment is 30 weeks (20 x $1^1\!/_2$), and this can be achieved only by employees aged between 62 and 64 with at least 20 years' service and whose normal retiring age is 65.

Once the number of pay-weeks has been established, this must then be multiplied by 'a week's pay' to produce the monetary sum. The statutory definition of a week's pay can be summarised as the contractual remuneration for working the normal weekly hours as at the calculation date. If there are no normal working hours (or if pay for a normal week fluctuates), then the average contractual remuneration over the 12 normal weeks of employment prior to the calculation date must be used. This raises three further matters for definition:

□ calculation date

□ contractual remuneration

□ normal working hours.

Calculation date

If pay has to be calculated by a 12-week average, the 12 weeks that must be taken are not the last 12 weeks in employment, but the 12 weeks counting backwards from the calculation date. The calculation date is the day on which *statutory* notice was given or was due. The pay rate to be used for employees with fixed salaries is also the pay rate at the calculation date – even if a pay rise is awarded between that date and the last day in employment. To illustrate this:

On 26 September an employee with five years' service is given five weeks' notice of redundancy, ending on 31 October. In September, her pay rate was £200 per week, but a national pay award increased this to £210 on 1 October. Her actual and statutory notice periods in this case are identical, and the calculation date is 26 September, so her redundancy payment will therefore be calculated on £200 per week, not the £210 which applied to her last four weeks of employment.

The purpose of the statute in defining the calculation date as an earlier date than the last day in employment was presumably to provide some protection against the possibility that normal hours or earnings might be cut once notice has been given.

Contractual remuneration

This is more than basic pay and covers any payments to which an employee is contractually entitled for work done. Typically it includes:

☐ shift allowances

☐ productivity bonuses

☐ piecework payments

☐ commission (eg on sales)

☐ performance or competence pay

☐ overtime, but only if this constitutes part of 'normal working hours'.

Not included are the value of payments in kind, expense payments, and benefits that are non-contractual (eg medical insurance subscriptions and most overtime).

Normal working hours

These are generally the hours expressly defined in the contract of employment and so normally exclude overtime. For example, if an employee's statement of terms and conditions says 'The hours of work are 39 per week', then for the purposes of statutory redundancy pay, the normal weekly working hours are 39, even if in the 12 weeks before the calculation date the employee has regularly worked a 45-hour week and been paid overtime. There are two exceptions:

☐ If the contractual hours include overtime, overtime is counted. This applies only if the overtime hours are guaranteed by the employer, and the employee is obliged to work them.

☐ If the contract does not specify the normal hours, then an implied normal working week has to be determined. This can be established only by examining the actual pattern of working and by deciding what a normal week consists of.

The final calculation

In cases other than those in which there is a fixed wage (eg where pay fluctuates because of bonuses), a week's pay must be calculated in the following way:

☐ Determine the correct 12-week period.

☐ Total the hours actually worked during the whole of this period. Include overtime hours – but at a plain rate (ie not enhanced by the equivalent of any overtime premium).

☐ Total all contractual remuneration (see above) received for this period but exclude the overtime premium (ie take the plain-time cost of overtime). Gross pay must be used in this calculation, not pay after tax and National Insurance deductions.

☐ Divide the total remuneration by the total hours to produce the average hourly rate.

☐ Determine the normal weekly working hours (ie excluding non-contractual overtime hours).

☐ Multiply the normal weekly hours by the average hourly rate to produce the normal week's pay.

☐ Check whether this is above or below the statutory maximum. If it is above, use the statutory maximum for the remaining calculations.

☐ Determine the employee's age and the number of full years of service within each of the three age-brackets 18 to 22, 23 to 40, and 41 and over.

☐ Working backwards from the current date, calculate the number of weeks' pay due for the statutory redundancy payment in each age-bracket.

☐ Multiply the total number of weeks' pay due by the amount of the week's pay (or the statutory maximum) to produce the full entitlement.

☐ Reduce this sum by the appropriate amount if the employee is between the ages of 64 and 65.

□ Give the employee written notification of the payment and how it has been calculated, and explain that these payments are tax-free.

Offsetting pension payments

A statutory regulation that is often either overlooked or not applied permits an employer to reduce the redundancy payment if a pension is paid to a redundant employee within 90 weeks of redundancy. The pension scheme must be approved as satisfactory by the Secretary of State for Employment and must guarantee a pension for life. The permitted scale of reductions to the redundancy payment is then worked out as follows:

□ If the pension is one-third or more of the employee's annual salary at the time of the redundancy, the redundancy payment can be waived completely.

□ If the pension is less than one-third of salary, the redundancy payment can be reduced by the proportion of one-third of salary that the annual pension is equivalent to. For example, if salary is £16,000 per annum and the pension is £4,000, the redundancy payment can be reduced by 75 per cent – because £4,000 is 75 per cent of £5,333 (one-third of salary).

An employer who wishes to apply these regulations – which are discretionary, not mandatory – must give the employee written notice of this intention together with full details of the calculations.

Non-statutory financial compensation

Many employers consider the statutory redundancy payments to be inadequate, particularly for employees whose pay is above the statutory weekly maximum. Many also consider it fair to make at least a modest payment to redundant employees with less than two years' service, who are excluded from the statutory scheme. For many organisations the statutory provisions are now treated as minimum, rather than standard, entitlements. There are, however, several exceptions:

□ Many very small companies say they cannot afford more than the statutory sums.

□ Companies in, or on the verge of, liquidation or insolvency may lack the finance to pay more than the statutory sums, or may even be unable to meet their statutory obligations.

□ Some industrial sectors – particularly those exposed to competitive tendering (eg contract cleaning and catering) rarely pay more than the statutory sums, except at times to managerial staff.

□ Local authorities have been barred by a Court of Appeal ruling from paying more than is permitted by the special local government statutory redundancy regulations.

The main variants among organisations that operate their own improved redundancy schemes are:

□ service-related schedules providing a standard amount of pay for each completed year of service, and sometimes, unlike the statutory scheme, part-sums for part-years. Schemes of this type do not always take age into account. Most provide between two weeks' and one month's pay per year of service, commonly subject to a maximum of between one and two years' salary. One industrial example uses the following formula:
   – two weeks' pay for each of the first five years' service
   – three weeks' pay for each of the next five years' service
   – four weeks' pay for each year's service after the first ten.

□ schedules adding a percentage or multiple to the statutory entitlement – generally by increasing the statutory sums by between 50 per cent and three times, with twice the statutory figure being the most common. In the following two company examples, one is age-related, the other is based on service:

Example 1
   – aged 18 to 49:   statutory sum plus 40 per cent
   – aged 50 to 64:   statutory sum plus 65 per cent

Example 2
   – 2 to 20 years' service: statutory sum plus 50 per cent
   – more than 20 years' service:
                           statutory sum plus 100 per cent

□ schedules using the statutory scheme's age and service criteria but waiving the statutory limit on a week's pay. There are also schemes that combine this and the previous formula.

There is no one best scheme or formula – except, perhaps, the principle that there should not be a salary limitation. Other than this, the right scheme for any organisation is one that best suits the nature of the business and the broader aspects of its employment style and policies. The IPD's approach is set out in the Institute's *Guide on Redundancy* (London, IPD, 1996):

> The IPD recommends higher levels of compensation if at all possible, as the statutory sums are often too small to compensate adequately for the loss of a job.

There are three important points to bear in mind when making redundancy payments above the statutory minima:

□ It is advisable, when giving employees written details of these payments, to state that they include the statutory entitlement and to state what this sum is. Without this clarification it is possible that an employee may make a tribunal claim for the statutory sum, arguing that the employer's payment was *ex gratia* and intended to be additional to any statutory entitlement.
□ Although redundancy compensation is normally payable tax-free, sums that exceed £30,000 (including aggregated sums of which a redundancy payment is only a part) do attract tax.
□ Part-timers should receive the pro rata equivalent of any extra redundancy payments made to full-timers.

Some employers pay monies additional to either statutory or their own better redundancy payments by always granting pay in lieu of notice. This is done in two ways:

□ by giving no notice – the questionable practice of effecting redundancy dismissals instantly without prior warning, as discussed in Chapter 5
□ by giving notice on a verbal and informal basis, but not confirming this formally and in writing until the last day of employment, and then still paying monies in lieu of notice – usually as a way of boosting tax-free payments.

Genuine payments in lieu of notice (as in the first instance, above) can be paid tax-free, because legally they constitute liquidated damages for a breach of contract – the failure to provide contractual notice. The somewhat artificial payments in the second instance are suspect from a tax viewpoint, because the Inland Revenue would challenge their validity as tax-free liquidated damages if it could be shown that notice had in fact been given.

There is another tax-trap if a right to notice payments of this kind is incorporated in individual contracts of employment or any other formal scheme that might be interpreted as giving employees a contractual right to them. Once a payment is contractual, it becomes taxable, so no reference should be made in any published documents or procedures to the payment of monies in lieu of notice if their tax-free status is to be preserved.

Other forms of compensation

Compensation for redundancy need not be limited to the payment of lump sums – indeed, some other methods of assistance may in some circumstances be more appreciated. Among these other measures are:

☐ for older employees, early retirement benefits such as an immediate pension, possibly with some enhancement to compensate in part for the lost years of contributions. The precise form of such arrangements depends on the nature of the pension scheme and the financial state of the pension fund, but may include crediting the employee with additional years' service, or using an additional lump-sum to purchase an annuity. One company links such payments to a schedule of age-related lump sums:
  - aged 18 to 21: one week's pay per year of service
  - aged 22 to 40: two weeks' pay per year of service
  - aged 41 to 64: three weeks' pay per year of service

If the employee uses this to purchase additional pension benefits, the company will add a sum equal to the employee's sum for this purpose.

☐ offering the redundant employee the opportunity of undertaking some work for the organisation on a consultancy or freelance basis. The employee's own work may have disappeared, but there may be an occasional requirement for some activities of a project nature for which an experienced ex-employee would be a better choice than a conventional commercial consultant. Providing cover for staff absences is another possibility.

☐ for employees with company cars, allowing them either to take over ownership or to purchase the vehicles at a discounted rate; or at least extending their use of the car for a significant period after the redundancy. To suddenly lose a car and have to commit a significant proportion of a redundancy sum to car purchase can be one of the worst immediate financial effects of redundancy for some staff.

☐ assisting the redundant employee to extend private medical insurance cover for a period after the redundancy. This is another benefit that, if withdrawn, can suddenly create financial problems. A phased withdrawal may ease this situation.

Other aspects of assistance and support for redundant employees are dealt with in Chapter 11.

Key points

☐ To be eligible for a statutory redundancy payment, an employee must have been dismissed.

☐ Employees are ineligible if they have less than two years' service.

☐ Service while aged between 16 and 18 does not count towards the two-year service criterion.

☐ Employees at or above their normal retiring age (or over 65 if there is no normal retiring age) are ineligible.

☐ Normal retiring age is either the contractual age for retirement (provided this is adhered to) or the age at which the category of employees concerned reasonably expect to retire.

☐ Service has to be continuous to count towards the two-year (or five-year) criterion.

☐ Service is deemed to be continuous unless the employer can prove otherwise.

☐ Breaks in service of less than one full week ending on a Saturday are discounted.

- Where the length of the working week is variable or in doubt, it is the normal (not average) week that must be used.
- Voluntary or non-contractual overtime does not count towards the length of the working week.
- Periods of absence while on strike do not break service but do not count towards length of service.
- If an employee leaves because of sickness and is re-engaged within 26 weeks, employment is treated as continuous.
- Redundancy payments are calculated on the basis of half a week's pay per year of service from the ages of 18 to 22, one week's pay between the ages of 22 and 40, and one and a half weeks' pay for service from the age of 41.
- Between the ages of 64 and 65, the payment is reduced by one-twelfth for each completed month.
- There is a maximum of 20 years' service.
- There is a maximum limit (revised annually) to a week's pay.
- Pay is calculated by reference to the calculation date – the date when statutory notice was due.
- Pay includes all contractual payments (such as bonuses) for work done – except overtime premia.
- If pay is variable, the average over the 12 weeks before the calculation date is used.
- Employees must be given a written statement of their redundancy payments.
- It is permissible to reduce the redundancy payment if a pension approved by the Secretary of State is paid within 90 weeks of the redundancy.
- Many employers pay more than the statutory sums – often waiving the statutory limit on a week's pay and paying at least double the statutory figure.
- When paying a larger sum, it should be stated in writing that this includes the statutory entitlement.
- The statutory sum is payable tax-free.
- Pay in lieu of notice is sometimes used to boost tax-free payments but cannot be paid tax-free if it has been specified as a contractual right.

☐ Other forms of non-statutory compensation include:
  – early retirement pensions with enhancements
  – providing work on a consultancy basis
  – allowing the employee to keep the company car
  – extending the period of private medical cover.

10 BUSINESS TRANSFERS AND FAILURES

Some of the most complicated aspects of redundancy in both legal and management terms occur when businesses become insolvent or when part or all of a business is sold or taken over by another organisation. Do redundancies occur automatically? How do employees get their redundancy money if their employer is insolvent? Are there circumstances in which redundancy dismissals resulting from a business transfer are unfair? Who should make the redundancy payments when a transfer occurs? These are just some of the many questions that can arise, and to which neither statute nor case-law always provides definitive answers.

This chapter does not attempt to provide a comprehensive guide to every employment aspect of business failures or transfers, but concentrates on the redundancy elements. To do so, it is necessary to provide some background information, although this should be taken as providing no more than pointers to factors on which, in any real-life situation, specialist legal advice should be sought. One expert commentator described the law on these subjects as a minefield which 'will inevitably catch out the parties to small-scale transfers who innocently believe their transaction to be a relatively simple one'.

There are four basic principles underlying the complexities that can arise in individual cases:

☐ If employees lose their jobs because of the failure of the organisation they have worked for, they are taken to have been dismissed on redundancy grounds, whether or not their employer has issued redundancy notices.

❑ If, in these circumstances, they are entitled to statutory redundancy payments that cannot be paid because the business is insolvent, they can apply to the DTI for payment.

❑ If an 'undertaking' is transferred from one employer to another, the terms of the contracts of employment of the transferred employees (except for pension provisions) have to be taken over by the receiving employer (the transferee), and there is no break in continuity of service. There is consequently no need for the old employer (the transferor) to terminate the employment contracts of the employees concerned on redundancy grounds, or for the transferee to offer new employment contracts.

❑ If, in these circumstances, either the transferor or transferee dismisses an employee for reasons connected with the transfer (including a redundancy dismissal), such a dismissal is automatically unfair and the legal obligation to make any redundancy and unfair-dismissal compensation payments then falls on the transferee – even if the redundancy dismissals were made by the transferor before the transfer.

To explain and expand on these principles, a number of different issues have to be considered. The principal issues to consider are:

❑ business transfers – general principles
❑ redundancies when the transfer regulations do not apply
❑ business failures
❑ takeovers and mergers
❑ consultation and trade union rights.

Business transfers – general principles

The set of statutory provisions that, in addition to the generality of employment legislation, influences the management of transfers of a business (or part of a business) from one organisation to another are the Transfer of Undertakings (Protection of Employment) Regulations 1981 (TUPE) and the case-law to which these complicated regulations have given rise. The regulations were introduced to meet the UK's obligation to honour the EU Acquired Rights Directive but have had to be amended several times because, as drafted originally, they failed fully to reflect the Directive's provisions. Initially restricted in the UK to transfers of commercial undertakings, they had later to be extended to cover the public sector. A UK limitation of consultation rights to trade unions has also been in conflict with the EU's requirement for consultation to be with employee representatives – the same situation that led to the inclusion of elected employee representatives in the general legislation on collective redundancy consultation.

The basic principles in the regulations that govern employees' rights and employers' obligations when a TUPE transfer occurs are these:

☐ The new employer in a transfer must take over the contracts of employment of the old employer's staff and so maintain their continuity of employment.

☐ Any dismissals, before or after the transfer, are automatically unfair if the reason for the dismissal is connected with the transfer.

☐ The exceptions to this are dismissals for 'economic, technical or organisational reasons entailing changes in the workforce' – which may be fair if they are decided and processed fairly and reasonably in accordance with general employment law.

☐ The new employer is ultimately responsible for any redundancy and unfair-dismissal compensation payments that may be caused by the transfer.

☐ Consultation must take place with the recognised trade unions or elected employee representatives for the employees affected by the transfer.

☐ The transferee must continue to apply the terms of collective agreements that relate to the transferred employees and to continue the recognition of the transferred employees' trade unions if the transferred undertaking retains its identity.

Although these principles may seem straightforward, there has been long-running uncertainty about the precise meaning of 'transfers', 'undertakings', 'economic, technical or organisational' and 'changes in the workforce', with a series of decisions by the UK courts and the ECJ about the interpretation of these terms in particular cases. Case-law is still being developed on these issues, so the following summary of what the legal position appears to be in early 1999 needs to be checked against later, leading case-law and amendments likely to be made to the regulations as a result of the government's consultations on possible revisions to the EU Directive.

What is an undertaking?

There is no problem with interpreting this part of the regulations when a whole business is sold or otherwise transferred to another business – using 'business' to cover not just private-sector commercial organisations but also those in the public and voluntary sectors. For example, a charity taken over by another charity would be an undertaking for the purposes of these regulations. Difficulties occur when only part of an undertaking is involved – for example, if a magazine publisher sells just one title to another publisher. Is such a sale (and transfer of business) covered by the regulations? The regulations specifically apply to parts of undertakings but, to be covered, these need to have certain characteristics. In a dispute, a tribunal or the courts look at all the facts of the particular case and have regard to such factors as whether assets are transferred and whether the activity or function involved is an 'economic entity' which retains its identity after the transfer.

What is a transfer?

For a transfer to occur, the key factor from an employment viewpoint is whether or not the transaction involves a change in the identity of the employer. There are complications, however, particularly in the field of contracting and sub-contracting where there are doubts as to whether the re-letting of a contract by a client to a new contractor constitutes a transfer between the old and new contractors. The legal position probably varies from case to case, depending on such factors as whether the new contractor takes over plant, premises or equipment used by the previous contractor, and whether he or she already has a workforce to handle the activity involved. The other main factor applying to all transfers is whether the work being done is substantially the same, before and after the transfer.

What are economic, technical or organisational reasons (ETO)?

A transferee can escape the penalties for dismissing employees if the reasons for such dismissals (normally redundancy) are for economic, technical or organisational reasons 'entailing changes in the workforce'. This may seem to open the door to wide-ranging evasion, but the courts have been very restrictive in their interpretations of ETO (as this element is widely termed). The phrase has to be set against the other element that makes any dismissal 'connected with' the transfer automatically unfair. In lay terms, this means that if employees are dismissed in order to help the transfer to take place, such dismissals are unfair, even though it could be argued that the reason was economic – ie to make the business more attractive to the potential buyer. In practice, ETO has been a factor related mainly to action taken by the transferee after the transfer has occurred. So an employer might initially accept all the transferor's employees on their existing pay rates, but shortly after the transfer either dismiss some to achieve cost reductions, or dismiss those who will not accept cuts in their pay and conditions. There have been cases where a transferee has been able to convince a tribunal that redundancies have been necessary on economic grounds soon after a transfer for reasons unconnected with the transfer itself – such as the loss of a contract or a deterioration in the company's trading situation. But despite two CA cases, there is still a lack of clarity about the practical application of ETO.

Changes in the workforce

ETO reasons only apply when they entail 'changes in the workforce'. This has been interpreted as meaning, in most cases, workforce reductions, though it could probably also apply to significant changes in the mix of jobs or skills. What this element of the regulations rules out is dismissing employees because they will not give up their previous contractual terms, even if there are pressing economic reasons for such a change.

Employee consultation

The regulations include a specific requirement for consultation with the employees affected by an impending transfer. These are separate from the collective consultation provisions described in Chapter 7, which apply to impending redundancies, although the principles are very similar. Trade unions or elected employee representatives must be given information and consulted about the:

☐ fact that a transfer is due to occur, its expected date, and the reasons for it

☐ 'legal, economic and social' implications of the transfer for those affected

☐ 'measures' that the transferor and transferee intend to take in relation to these employees.

The consultation must be genuine and be conducted with a view to reaching agreement. It must apply to all the employees likely to be affected by the transfer, and this can include those in both organisations whose work (or other aspects of their jobs) may change because of new working arrangements made necessary by the transfer. There has been legal argument about the meaning of 'measures', but a common-sense approach has been adopted by the courts to indicate that the word covers anything about the arrangements for implementing the transfer for which it is reasonable for employees to have an interest or concerns.

Managing a TUPE transfer

There may be doubts in any particular case as to whether or not a transfer is bound by TUPE, but it is not unusual for the two employers involved to agree to handle a transfer as though TUPE did apply. TUPE principles go a long way towards meeting the very real worries employees have when they learn that another organisation is about to take over their work. The immediate fear is of job losses. Even if they are then given assurances about employment with the new employer, there may still be concern about the terms and conditions the new employer will offer.

It is normally in both parties' interests for employees' concerns to be recognised and addressed constructively, particularly if the success of the transfer is dependent on the new employer acquiring the skills and experience of the existing workforce. One risk, if fears about the transfer are not allayed, is that key staff will obtain other employment and the transferee will then be left with an inadequate workforce to handle the incoming work. There is also the legal risk for the transferee of having to pay compensation for any redundancies effected by the transferring employer, even if the transferee had no part and no knowledge of them. The old employer may not seem to have the same degree of potential risk, but a badly managed transfer may damage the morale of the remaining employees and perhaps put them under untenable working pressure if the impact of the transfer on the work of the non-transferred staff has not been given adequate attention.

For all these reasons, most transfers are best implemented on the basis of a project plan jointly evolved and managed by the two employers involved. The components of this plan may include:

☐ issuing to all employees of both organisations full information about the transfer, the reasons for it and what it will mean for employees in both organisations. It is important that this information is given to staff not directly involved, as well as to those due for transfer. Without this widespread information, there are likely to be ill-informed rumours and unnecessary concerns among staff at large.

☐ the provision of full information to the transferee about the pay and conditions of staff due for transfer. The potential new employer will need to know well in advance about the costs being incurred and be able to consider the impact within the receiving workforce of new colleagues who are probably employed on different terms.

☐ giving employees due for transfer an opportunity to be addressed by and ask questions of their potential managers. It can also be helpful to arrange for these employees to visit their potential new workplace in advance of the transfer.

☐ providing, in unionised organisations, full information to the trade unions in both organisations, together with genuine consultations about any matters of interest or concern. In the absence of trade unions, employees can be invited to elect their own representatives for this collective consultation.

- ☐ ensuring that employees due for transfer (those employed wholly or mainly on the function to be transferred) understand that if they refuse to transfer they will not be able to claim redundancy compensation
- ☐ issuing (as a matter of good practice) each incoming employee with a letter welcoming them to the new organisation and confirming their contractual position, and giving them any relevant information about their new working arrangements – although new contracts of employment do not have to be issued to the staff who are transferring (because their existing contractual conditions and continuity of employment are preserved)
- ☐ beyond this, a full range of induction for the transferred staff
- ☐ giving careful consideration to the pension position of the transferred staff. Pension rights are not protected by TUPE, but because of their importance, the two organisations should review any differences between their two pension schemes and do whatever is practicable to avoid the transferred staff experiencing a significant worsening of their pension benefits.

There are two matters that the transferor needs to guard against before the transfer takes effect. The first is succumbing to pressure from the transferee to terminate someone's employment whom the new employer would rather not employ. There is a high risk of any such dismissal – whether described as redundancy or for some other reason – being unfair, because it would have been made in connection with the transfer. Secondly, redundancies made in order to reduce the cost of the function due for transfer (and therefore its price if put up for sale) are also likely to be ruled as unfair for the same reason. There are situations, however, in which redundancies made shortly before or after the transfer would meet the criterion of being for genuine business reasons unconnected with the transfer. In such cases, the normal redundancy procedures as described in previous chapters should be followed – although it would also be advisable to ensure that adequate documentary evidence was available to show they were unrelated to the transfer.

Redundancies to which the transfer regulations do not apply

If a transaction involving some form of transfer does not fall within the TUPE regulations, the contracts of employment of the employees concerned are terminated – whether or not the employees are re-engaged by the new owner or employer. In effect, such termination constitutes a redundancy dismissal and, if handled in accordance with the standard procedures, such dismissals are not unfair and redundancy payments would then be due. These can be avoided, however, by arranging for the new employer to offer employment to the employees whose work is being transferred. Those who accept and start work with the transferee within four weeks of losing their old jobs are then taken to have continuous service. In other words, the position is the same as for employees who are made redundant but offered alternative work within their own organisation. The practical points for the transferor to bear in mind when managing this process are as follows:

❑ Discuss and agree with the transferee what procedure is to be followed regarding offers of employment to the employees. For example, it might be made a condition of sale that the new employer interviews all the employees concerned with a view to offering continued employment.

❑ Arrange for the new employer to decide about and make such offers before the date of the transfer. Check that the transferee understands that the standard trial period of four weeks applies to employees who accept these offers.

❑ Explain the situation to staff (and their trade unions or employee representatives) and inform them about their employment rights, pointing out that if they accept offers of employment from the new employer their continuity of employment will be maintained. Also, explain the position regarding redundancy payments, emphasising that the unreasonable refusal of a suitable offer of employment with the new employer would disqualify them from redundancy compensation. It may be necessary to stress that a refusal based solely on an objection to the change of employer is not a sufficient reason.

❑ Ensure the transferee provides full information about the

offers made and accepted or rejected, together with the starting dates of those employees who accept. Without this information, the transferor will not know which employees are entitled to redundancy payments.

☐ Decide and implement redundancy dismissals and payments for those employees who are not offered jobs or who reasonably reject unsuitable offers.

Circumstances may arise in which the old employer makes a redundancy payment but the employee concerned later accepts employment with the transferee within the necessary timescale to acquire continuity of service. There is no question of recovering the payment in such cases. The result is simply that the employee loses continuity of service so far as entitlement to redundancy rights are concerned – though not for other rights.

Business failures

Insolvency situations are the cause of many transfers. The exact state of the organisation – whether it has reached the stage of administration, receivership or liquidation – can affect the employees' ability to enforce their rights and benefits.

A situation in which the employer simply reduces the number of staff to bring down the wage bill is a classic case of redundancy, and the employer will be liable for any redundancy, unfair dismissal, wages in lieu of notice or other payments to the employee. If the employer facing financial difficulties decides to sell off part of the business and there is a transfer of that part of the business, TUPE will apply, and the acquiring employer will become liable for any outstanding debts in relation to the contract.

Under the Insolvency Act 1986 the company's directors may propose an arrangement or composition to the creditors. This may involve the restructuring of the company, and it must be approved by both the shareholders and the creditors. If staff are dismissed, part of the business transferred to a third party, business transferred from one group company to another, or subsidiaries merged, then the redundancy provisions and TUPE will apply in the normal way.

Administration

The Insolvency Act 1986 introduced the concept of administration in order to provide organisations in financial difficulties with a period of time free from legal action during which to put their affairs in order under the management of an administrator appointed by the court. This is granted only when at least part of the organisation may be rescued. The powers of the administrator include running the business, closing or selling parts of the business and transferring parts to subsidiaries (see 'hiving down' below), as well as entering into arrangements and compositions with creditors. There is no change of employer upon the appointment of an administrator, and so liability for redundancy, unfair dismissal etc remains. Sales or transfers, however, are likely to fall within TUPE.

Receivership

The debenture-holders, who provide long-term loans to the company (normally in return for fixed or floating charges on the assets), can appoint a receiver. The receiver's aim is to realise the company's assets for the benefit of the debenture-holders – not for the benefit of the company. The receiver is appointed as a manager of the company and, unless appointed by the court, acts on behalf of the company. The company is therefore liable for the redundancy, unfair dismissal and other liabilities stemming from the actions of the receiver. However, under the Insolvency Act 1986 the receiver is personally liable on employment contracts adopted by him or entered into by him in the course of his duties. Although the receiver becomes personally liable it does not follow that he becomes the employer or that any transfer of the business has occurred.

Liquidation

A liquidator is appointed to wind up a company. The company may be wound up voluntarily by the shareholders – but only when it can pay all its debts – or it may be wound up compulsorily either by court order upon a petition of its creditors or directors or simply by order of the court itself. The most common ground for a compulsory winding-up is a company's inability to pay its debts.

The legal position of the liquidator depends on the type of

liquidation. If there is a voluntary liquidation, the liquidator is an agent acting on behalf of the company, and so the employees remain the liability of the company. On the other hand, when the liquidator is appointed by the court he acts on behalf of the court. Employment with the company ceases and the employees are subsequently employed by the liquidator, who will then be liable for any dismissals that take place.

Consultation

Recent cases have decided that the statutory collective consultation requirements still apply, even when a company is in administration or receivership or is insolvent. These circumstances do not meet the criterion of being so unexpected and sudden as to make consultation with trade unions or employee representatives impossible.

Transfer rights

Whenever a transfer of a business has occurred, the rights of the employees will be affected by TUPE. In particular, the restructuring of an undertaking or group may take place in several stages, in which case the several transactions may be treated as one. In deciding whether they should be treated as one, a tribunal will take into account the time-lapse between the transactions and the extent to which the transferor and transferee controlled the relevant part before the final transaction. So if an employer transfers the assets to one subsidiary, leaving the staff employed by another company, and then sells the assets to the acquiring organisation, leaving them to select the staff to whom they will offer employment (known as 'hiving down'), this could well amount to a series of transactions. If so, then all the staff employed immediately before each transaction will be treated as employed immediately before the last transaction and at that point will be able to enforce any rights they may have under TUPE.

Avoiding rights under TUPE by hiving down is permitted only in very limited circumstances, applying to a hiving-down undertaken by a receiver, an administrator appointed under the Insolvency Act 1986, or the liquidator in the case of a creditors' winding-up. TUPE permits the business (or part of it) to be transferred to a wholly owned subsidiary of the company, and provides that the regulations will apply only when that subsidiary ceases to be wholly owned (for example, upon sale or transfer of the shares to another organisation) or when the business is transferred to another organisation (for example, the business itself is purchased, rather than shares in the owning subsidiary). The effect of this is that the only employees who obtain rights under TUPE are those employed immediately before the final transaction. Of course, dismissals taking place at this stage could be dismissals justified for an ETO reason.

Insolvency

When an employer is unable to pay statutory redundancy benefit owing to insolvency, employees may apply to the Secretary of State (DTI) for payment. Where the employer is a person, insolvency covers situations in which bankruptcy has been declared or a deceased's estate is being administered as an insolvent estate. Where the employer is a company, insolvency applies when:

- that company is subject to a winding-up order or an order of administration
- it has entered into a voluntary arrangement under the Insolvency Act 1986
- a resolution for a voluntary winding-up has been passed
- a receiver or manager has been appointed by the debenture-holders
- debenture-holders have entered into possession of the property.

Where none of these have occurred, employees do not have to actually prove insolvency but must show that they have taken reasonable steps, short of legal action, to obtain payment and that the employer has refused to pay or has not in fact paid. There is a similar provision for other payments due to the employee, namely:

- arrears of pay, to a maximum of eight weeks
- pay for the statutory period of notice
- up to six weeks' holiday pay
- any basic award of compensation for unfair dismissal

◻ reimbursement of the fees paid by apprentices or articled clerks.

These rights are enforced by employment tribunals. The procedure for employees to follow is as follows – and should be explained by any responsible employer:

◻ Make a written application for a redundancy payment to the local office of the DTI. It is helpful to call at the office to collect the necessary documentation.

◻ The application must be made within six months of the date of dismissal.

◻ Within the application, provide evidence either that the employer has been approached for payment and has failed or refused to pay, or evidence that the employer is insolvent. An employer is insolvent if, as an individual, he or she has been declared bankrupt, or if, as a company, a receiver has been appointed or the company is subject to a winding-up order.

◻ Provide evidence of entitlement to a statutory redundancy payment – ie details of age and service that meet the normal criteria for continuous service and age limits.

◻ Note that if the DTI refuses to pay, the employee concerned can pursue a claim against the Department through an employment tribunal.

It is also possible for an employer in financial difficulties to apply to the DTI for assistance in meeting the costs of statutory redundancy compensation. The DTI has to be provided with full details of the reasons for any such application, supported by copies of the company's accounts and any other information required to establish whether or not it would be possible for the company to fund the redundancy payments.

Takeovers and mergers

One of the most traumatic events for many employees occurs when a public limited company is taken over as a consequence of another organisation acquiring a majority shareholding, or a merger is arranged through changes in shareholdings. This has often led to asset sales, major reorganisations, the introduction of differences in employment style and conditions, and some-times large-scale redundancies – in short, to many actions that would be contrary to the various legal requirements outlined in this chapter. Yet none of the legal provisions described in this chapter apply in these circumstances.

To the lay observer it may well seem odd that a company that acquires another by purchasing shares (perhaps in the context of a hostile takeover bid) is free from specific transfer regulations, whereas the acquisition of a business activity by direct purchase is subject to the complexities of TUPE. The reason is that when a business is taken over through share-purchasing, there is no change in the legal identity of the company as a corporate body. The fact that there has been a change among the shareholders does not in law make the company a new employer, because the employees continue to be employed on their existing contracts by the same company. If the new majority shareholders, through their directors and managers, wish to make major changes to the workforce, they are bound by the same general employment legislation and contract law as any other company. In other words, so far as redundancy is concerned, a company after a takeover should follow the same procedures and meet the same obligations as has been described in earlier chapters. There are no special provisions.

Key points

☐ If employees lose their jobs because of business failures, they are entitled to redundancy payments – provided the standard age and service criteria are met.

☐ If an employer will not or cannot make redundancy pay-ments in these circumstances, employees can apply to the DTI for payment. Employers in financial difficulty can also apply to the DTI for assistance in paying redundancy com-pensation.

☐ If an undertaking is transferred from one employer to another, the new employer (the transferee) has to take over the employees' contracts of employment unchanged. Pensions are not included in this requirement. The new employer must also continue to give effect to any relevant collective agreements. There is no redundancy, and employees maintain continuity of employment.

☐ For a transaction to come within the transfer regulations it must involve a change of employer and be of an activity or function that has a distinct identity which it retains after the transfer.

☐ If either the transferor or transferee dismisses an employee for reasons connected with the transfer (eg simply to make the transaction more commercially attractive), this will be automatically unfair.

☐ Dismissals (redundancies) effected fairly and reasonably for ETO reasons are not unfair.

☐ The ultimate legal responsibility for meeting redundancy payments for redundancies implemented before the transfer, and for any related unfair dismissal compensation, lies with the transferee.

☐ The recognised trade unions or elected employee representatives must be informed of, and consulted about, any impending transfer.

☐ The penalty for failing to inform or consult with the trade unions is a payment of up to four weeks' pay to each of the affected employees.

☐ In a transaction that does not fall within the transfer regulations, the contracts of the employees of the transferor are terminated, the employees are entitled to redundancy payments and there is no statutory requirement for the transferee to offer them employment.

☐ However, if the transferee offers employment before an employee's job with the transferor ends, and the employee accepts, no redundancy payment need be made, provided the employee starts the new job within four weeks of the old job ending.

☐ If, in these circumstances, an employee unreasonably rejects a suitable offer by the transferee, the entitlement to a redundancy payment is lost.

☐ Takeovers and mergers effected through changes in shareholdings are not covered by the transfer legislation, because there is no change in the identity of the employing company as a corporate employer.

11 CARING FOR REDUNDANT EMPLOYEES

Any organisation that accepts that its responsibility towards its workforce extends beyond the minimum requirements of employment legislation will do more for employees who lose their jobs through redundancy than just provide financial compensation. In the words of the *IPD Guide on Redundancy* (IPD, 1996):

> Redundancy is a traumatic experience, often resulting in a loss of self-esteem and generating serious anxiety about financial security and future employability. Even the most confident of employees can be very badly affected by redundancy and need advice and support in accepting the realities of the situation and mounting an effective job search.

The organisation that does this is not only meeting its moral obligations, it is also enhancing its reputation as a good

Type of assistance	Employee category			
	Senior manage-ment	Other manage-ment	White collar	Blue collar
Payments beyond statutory minima	96	95	95	95
Provision of outplacement services	63	48	38	29
Personal financial planning	47	39	36	31
Extended use of company car	44	25	8	3
Acting as a consultant for a period	32	9	5	2
Continuation of medical benefits	32	19	12	6
Secretarial help in job search	24	21	18	11
Continuation of life assurance	21	17	15	11
Use of office space in job search	18	14	11	7
Continuation of subsidised mortgage	11	10	10	5

employer among its own remaining employees and in the outside world.

A 1992 survey of redundancy practices in over 500 private- and public-sector organisations showed the percentages of employers providing various forms of redundancy assistance listed in the table on page 184.

These results are probably skewed towards organisations that take a responsible and comprehensive approach to assisting their employees in a redundancy situation. But although the detailed figures may not be fully representative of general practice, they do show the predominance of enhanced compensation payments and the extensive use made of outplacement services. They also show that the more senior the employee, the wider the range of assistance – a situation not wholly consistent with an even-handed approach to meeting redundant employees' needs. In many cases, it is the less-skilled blue-collar employee who suffers most from redundancy.

Chapter 9 dealt with redundancy payments and other forms of economic assistance, such as pension enhancements and the extended use of company cars. Reference has also been made in Chapter 7 to action that an employer may take to help redundant employees find alternative employment – through job shops, for example, and by contacts between the organisation and other employers. This chapter therefore concentrates on redundancy counselling, both in-house and provided through external outplacement services.

Counselling: general principles

A distinction can be drawn between two aspects of redundancy counselling:

☐ helping employees understand and come to terms with the fact that they have lost their jobs

☐ the provision of specific advice and assistance with personal financial planning, career replanning, and job search.

Although in practice, these two aspects may be taken together, the distinction is important. Few people can apply themselves to a vigorous and well-planned job-search programme until they have accepted the reality of their situation and have put initial feelings of resentment, anger or fear behind them. Excellent advice about finances, CVs or retraining opportunities will have little impact on someone still seething with emotion after learning of his or her redundancy.

Handling the first stage of redundancy counselling requires considerable skill and should not be attempted by anyone who does not, as a minimum, understand the general principles of all forms of counselling. Ideally, it is a task for the trained counsellor or for the personnel manager equipped with specialist training in counselling skills. There are many pitfalls for the well-intentioned but unskilled person who attempts to provide redundancy counselling in the preparatory phase, and these include:

☐ placing too much emphasis on expressions of sympathy. Saying how sorry you are about the person's loss of employment does little to help that person come to terms with the situation, and may even exacerbate feelings of resentment. A typical response may well be 'If *you're* sorry, how do you think *I* feel!' or 'If you're as sorry as that, why have you made me redundant?'

☐ repeating such well-known clichés as 'Look on it as an opportunity.' The idea is sound, but it needs to be developed and drawn out of the employee in a way specific to the situation – not quoted as generally received wisdom

☐ arguing with the employee who makes accusations of unfairness or who questions the necessity for redundancy

☐ taking 'ownership' of the solutions to the employee's problems by being far too directive about what he or she should do. Counselling is not a matter of thinking or acting for the counselled employee, or of imposing solutions.

The aim of redundancy counselling is to help those counselled to make a personal assessment of their situation and evolve their own plans of action. It requires an ability to see the situation from other people's viewpoint, but this does not imply making decisions on their behalf. To quote one counselling expert:

Counselling is a mechanism for building self-reliance in an individual by assisting them to make decisions. . . The support should be given without it becoming a crutch or encouraging dependence.

One of the keys to effective counselling is to encourage the employee to talk – and initially this may involve listening to an emotional outburst. The existence of anger or resentment needs to be recognised and dealt with. Unless it is brought into the open, it is likely to continue as an inhibiting factor, preventing the employee from taking a positive approach to any job search. The experienced counsellor may well begin a counselling session with the simple question 'Tell me how you feel about things' or 'What were your reactions when you were first told about your redundancy?' The result may sometimes be some extreme and antagonistic statements about the organisation or about particular senior managers. The good counsellor does not respond by arguing, however tempting it may be to dispute such comments. The aim is to release the emotion so that the discussion can move on to a more constructive phase, and what needs to be displayed at this point is understanding rather than argument – or even sympathy. So one response might be along these lines: 'I'm not surprised that you feel that way: I don't necessarily agree with everything you've said but I understand why you've said it. Now, what thoughts do you have about the future, because that is what we really need to talk about?'

Counselling: in-house or by external specialist?

Given that counselling requires particular skills, should the untrained generalist personnel or line manager attempt it, or should outside professional assistance be sought through the use of an outplacement service? It is impractical to suggest that every case be referred externally, and in any event, personnel managers should acquire some expertise in counselling, whether or not there is an immediate need for this in relation to redundancy. Counselling skills are called for in a number of other situations, such as in the handling of grievances, complaints about harassment, and various welfare issues.

There is also a distinction to be drawn between the first time an employee is notified of redundancy and a full-scale counselling session. Chapters 5 and 7 discussed the handling of redundancy notification and consultation, and this must always be undertaken by the employee's line or personnel manager. It is rarely good practice to plunge straight into a counselling session immediately after telling the bad news. The employee may be in a state of shock and will probably benefit far more if counselling occurs a short time after the first notification. What can be arranged at the initial stage is an appointment for later counselling – and this might be either with the personnel manager or with an outside consultant.

The advantages of using an external counselling or outplacement service are these:

☐ The employee may talk more freely to someone outside the organisation who has had no part in the redundancy decision.

☐ The outside specialist should be trained in counselling skills and have significant experience in handling redundancy counselling.

☐ If it is intended to use an external service for specific advice and assistance (eg CV-preparation, training in being interviewed), initial general counselling by the same specialist can establish a useful rapport which will contribute to the success of the whole process.

☐ The specialist outplacement consultancy can provide a range of information and services which few employers have available in-house.

☐ If it is to be effective, counselling cannot be rushed or kept within rigid time-limits. The busy generalist personnel manager may have too little time to handle a redundancy counselling session in a sufficiently relaxed manner.

There are some opposing arguments in support of keeping counselling in-house:

☐ There is a risk that, by referring redundancy cases to an external specialist, the impression may be given that the organisation is opting out of its responsibilities.

☐ It cannot be assumed that the staff of an outplacement consultancy are all professionally trained counsellors. In the most reputable consultancies this will be the case, but there are several hundred organisations offering outplacement services, and by no means all meet the high professional standards that a sensitive function of this kind requires.

□ The external counsellor may not fully understand the impact of the employing organisation's culture on employees' attitudes and expectations, and will not have detailed knowledge of the skills and aptitudes they have displayed in their work – information that may be vital to ensuring the relevance of career advice.

□ There is a cost for the use of outplacement services – generally 15 per cent of the employee's annual salary plus a flat-rate administration payment of between £1,000 and £2,000 for individual counselling. An outplacement programme in which a number of employees are given advice and assistance on a group basis will cost far less per head, although this would exclude intensive individual counselling and assistance.

Selecting an outplacement consultant

If it is decided to use an outplacement consultancy, great care should be taken in the selection. The IPD has a code of conduct for career and outplacement consultants, and prospective consultants can be asked whether they have formally adopted this code. Many of the major consultancies have also produced their own codes of ethics and exclude from their association any firm that takes private fee-paying clients – as distinct from corporate contracts. Apart from ensuring whether a consultant works within a professional code, the main points to check are these:

□ Prior to concluding a contract, will the consultant – without charge to and without commitment on the part of the prospective client – attend a meeting of sufficient duration to ensure a clear understanding is reached about the nature of the employees to be assisted, the specific requirements of the client, and (by the client) the expertise available within the consultancy?

□ What range of services and support can the consultant provide for the employees concerned?

- What premises does the consultant operate from, and what facilities are provided there for the client's employees?
- Have the consultants been trained in counselling skills? What other qualifications and experience do they have? (The IPD code says that consultants should be trained counsellors, have corporate membership of the Institute or be able to meet the necessary criteria for such membership, or have a relevant qualification in psychology.)
- For how long will support be provided to the employees? For full-cost outplacement, the consultant should continue support until the employee finds and starts another job – regardless of how long this might be.
- If the consultant also operates a search-and-selection business, what guarantees are there that outplacement advice will not be biased towards the additional fee-earning opportunities for the consultancy of placing the employee with an executive-search client?
- What arrangements will be made to provide the client with progress reports about the displaced employees' job searches?
- How are the consultancy fees to be paid? Will the consultant accept a contract in which a final stage payment is made only on the successful completion of the employee's job search?
- Will the consultant charge for any expenses in addition to the basic fees?

Outplacement services

A full-cost outplacement assignment for employees such as senior managers who are to be counselled and supported individually should include all the services listed below. There may be employees for whom some of these services are not needed, but the professionally competent outplacement consultancy will be able to offer the full range. This list of activities also serves as a checklist for organisations handling redundancy counselling in-house of the different types of assistance that employees who have been made redundant may find helpful.

- *Initial counselling.* The preliminary process of discharging any destructive emotional reaction and developing a positive attitude to the necessary adjustments to personal and career plans.

❏ *Financial advice*. Advising the employee about issues such as investment of the redundancy lump sum, pensions, social security payments, debt management and other financial implications of redundancy. Advice on the choice of pension options must, by law, be given only by registered investment advisers, and the best consultancies retain qualified specialist advisers to handle this aspect. Personnel managers who assist redundant employees in-house need to be very careful about giving financial advice. As well as possibly breaking the law about the provision of specific pensions advice, the whole topic really requires specialist knowledge if more is to be done than merely highlight matters for the redundant employee to research on his or her own account. It is feasible, of course, to obtain the services of a specialist adviser solely for this purpose, or to put the employee in contact with a firm of registered and independent financial advisers.

❏ *Skills analysis*. Helping employees to make an in-depth assessment of their experience, skills and competencies in order to have a clear view of the range of alternative work for which they may be suited, and of their most marketable attributes. It is often helpful for employees to begin this analysis by listing their specific achievements at work, and noting the types of work or organisation in which they feel they have been most (or least) successful.

❏ *Job focus*. On the basis of the skills analysis, clarifying the type and level of work (and type of organisation) on which a job search should concentrate. One consultant's manual encourages the employee to summarise the outcome of the skills analysis and job focus under three headings:
  – Main skills:
      according to track record
      according to preference
  – Preferred location:
      geographic
      economic sector/industry
      type/size of organisation
  – Level
      of responsibility
      of salary.

Consultants will normally advise the employee not only to think very broadly in the first instance but also to consider alternatives to paid employment, such as full-time higher education or self-employment. The effective consultant is able to provide detailed information and guidance on such alternatives – advice that may be difficult to provide through in-house outplacement because the organisation may well lack comprehensive knowledge in these fields.

☐ *CV-preparation.* Advising the employee on the production of a CV for use in job applications and in seeking interviews with potentially useful contacts. Some outplacement consultants persuade employees to use a standardised CV format, others encourage employees to design their own CVs, with guidance about content and style. The latter approach is preferable, because many experienced personnel managers are able to recognise the standard formats and immediately deduce that the application has been prepared with considerable assistance from a consultant. It is also good advice that CVs should be tailored to the particular job or organisation, rather than using the same document for all purposes.

☐ *Targeting organisations.* Assisting the employee to identify organisations in which opportunities may occur that match the results of the skills analysis and job focus. For managerial and professional-level jobs, most consultants emphasise that only a minority of private-sector vacancies are advertised on the open market. They therefore advocate approaches being made – either directly or through personal contacts – to all those organisations that either match the employee's focused aspirations or operate relevant search-and-selection consultancies. To help identify these organisations, the reputable consultancy will have available all the relevant reference material and directories, and probably maintain its own computerised database. This is one aspect of outplacement that is difficult for employers to supply in-house, because very few organisations stock a full range of trade and other directories or can readily undertake desk-research into the nature, size and status and key managers of tens of thousands of potential employers, private and public.

☐ *Making contacts.* Advising the employee on how best to break into the hidden market of unadvertised job opportunities.

Outplacement consultants advise employees to make full use of all known contacts (previous colleagues, suppliers or customers, family connections), either by asking directly about vacancies or by seeking these contacts' assistance in widening their contact network and spreading the news about their availability. Advice is given about telephone techniques for speaking to influential contacts and about writing speculative application letters. For managerial staff, more emphasis is placed on establishing contacts than on cold applications. Some consultants advise employees to by-pass personnel departments in making these contacts and to attempt to speak directly to relevant senior line managers.

□ *Replying to advertisements*. Advising the employee about the drafting of letters replying to advertisements and about the completion of application forms. The consultant will normally discuss a draft reply (or a provisionally completed application form) with the employee and suggest how improvements might be made. The emphasis is on highlighting strengths relevant to the job advertised.

□ *Interview skills*. Coaching the employee in the skills required when being interviewed. This is often one of the main activities in an outplacement assignment, the consultant conducting role-played interviews with the employee recorded on video and played back to assist in the learning process. Awkward and commonly asked questions are discussed and answers rehearsed. The importance of interview preparation is stressed, including the value of conducting some research on the organisation concerned so that intelligent responses can be made, and questions asked at the end of the interview that demonstrate knowledge and interest. Few busy personnel managers handling outplacement counselling in-house have the time to devote several hours of individual coaching to this one form of assistance.

□ *Salary negotiation*. Advising the employee how to handle the discussion of salary if he or she is successful in an application for a job for which the salary is negotiable. The consultant's manual referred to earlier makes several suggestions about this, including:

  – trying to avoid being the first to volunteer a salary indication

- never giving a single figure: always quote a range
- never talking of salary needs: always talk of the worth of the job
- always asking about salary increases – reviews, bonuses and the like
- not accepting or rejecting an offer on the spot: take time to consider it.

☐ *Managing the job search*. Encouraging the employee to treat searching for a job as a planned and managed process. Employees are often advised to develop a routine, with daily and weekly scanning of advertisements, time scheduled for writing contact letters and making telephone calls, and records maintained of targeted organisations and the date and result of every application.

☐ *Office facilities*. The provision of secretarial, typing, photo-copying and telephone facilities to support the job search, together with access to relevant reference and research material – directories, journals etc. Facilities of this kind, which are of a high standard and maintain confidentiality, are often easier to provide externally than in-house.

☐ *Follow-up*. Some consultants extend their support beyond the point at which an employee obtains another job and offer follow-up support for a short period. Should the employee experience difficulty in settling in to the new job, the consultant provides confidential counselling. If the new appointment proves unsuccessful within, say, a three-month period, the consultant may recommence general job-search support.

Other agencies

As well as commercial outplacement consultants, there are several non-profit-making organisations whose help can be obtained in providing assistance to redundant employees – particularly those in older age groups. The Pre-Retirement Association offers consultancy and training services to employers who wish to help employees with information and advice about every aspect of retirement – issues of great importance to the older redundant employee. REACH is a registered charity which finds part-time, expenses-only work for retired business or professional men and women who want to give some of their time to voluntary organisations with charitable aims. The older but active redundant executive who no longer wishes to have full-time paid employment (or who finds it impossible to secure such work) may well be helped to maintain a sense of worth by undertaking valuable voluntary work. Many colleges of further and higher education also run pre-retirement or similar courses, or will contribute to in-house courses of this kind.

Whichever approach is followed – in-house support, external outplacement or a mixture of in-house and externally contributed assistance – it is essential to ensure the accuracy and relevance of the information and advice given to employees experiencing redundancy. Some employees are, of course, entirely able to face the situation and take effective action with no assistance whatsoever. Many others will initially feel wholly at a loss as to how to proceed – or may waste much time, money and mental effort making poorly prepared applications to numerous unsuitable organisations. The help needed by vulnerable people in this traumatic period should be of the highest quality, and this is no task for amateurs, however well intended. However, handled with sensitivity and skill, in-house or external outplacement assistance can do much to minimise the adverse impact of redundancy and may, in some cases, be the route to positive improvements in a person's career development. For the personnel or line manager who has had the task of telling someone of his or her impending redundancy, contributing to that person's success in making a good career move also provides some satisfaction to offset the unpleasantness of redundancy implementation.

Key points

☐ Responsible employers provide redundancy counselling to assist employees in coping with redundancy and to help them find alternative employment.

☐ There are two aspects to counselling: initial general help in coming to terms with job losses, and guidance on specific issues such as personal finance and job search.

☐ General counselling requires specific counselling skills.

☐ A major fault in unskilled counselling is to create dependency on the counsellor rather than building self-reliance.

☐ Advantages of using external outplacement services include independence, specialist knowledge and expertise, and comprehensive support and facilities.

☐ Disadvantages include the impression that the employer is opting out of responsibility for the task, a risk of inadequately trained consultants, and cost.

☐ When selecting an outplacement consultant, enquiry should be made about the consultant's qualifications and training, the range and duration of support, the facilities provided, the consultancy's independence from search-and-selection, the provision of progress reports, and the calculation and timing of payment of fees.

☐ Outplacement services may include:
  – initial counselling
  – financial advice
  – skills analysis
  – identifying the type and location of possible new jobs
  – CV-preparation
  – identifying target organisations for job search
  – availability of directories, journals etc.
  – advice on making contacts
  – advice on replying to job advertisements
  – training in being interviewed
  – advice on negotiating salary within a job offer
  – advice on managing/recording the job-search process
  – office facilities for typing, telephoning and research
  – follow-up support after a new job has been taken.

☐ Group outplacement services can be provided for multiple redundancies.

12 SOURCES OF FURTHER INFORMATION

Books and leaflets

The Institute of Personnel and Development (IPD)

Redundancy. London, IPD, 1999. One of the IPD's *Legal Essentials* series, with up-to-date legal advice from the Institute's employment-law advisers, Hammond Suddards, including recent examples from case-law, checklists and policy guidelines. Contains chapters on consulting with employees, qualifying for redundancy pay (including statutory formulae and calculations), and how employers can get it wrong.

Transfer of Undertakings. London, IPD, 1999. In the same series as the above title, with information on the vital issues in the area, including the effect of legislation on the individual and collective agreements, the obligation to inform and consult, and warranties and indemnities, with practical examples.

The IPD Guide on Redundancy. London, IPD, 1996. One in a series of IPD guides to good people-management practice. Update due September 1999.

Redundancy: Key Facts Sheet. London, IPD, 1996 (revised 1998). Available free from the Communications Department.

TUPE: Information Note No. 15. London, IPD, 1998. Available from Library Information Services.

The Department of Trade and Industry (DTI)

Several relevant factsheets and leaflets are published by the DTI; call their orderline on 0870 1502 500 or visit their website at www.dti.gov.uk. (Readers may also like to know that the Redundancy Payments Service operates a Freephone Helpline on 0500 848 489.)

- ☐ *Facing Redundancy: Time off for job-hunting or to arrange training.*
- ☐ *Guarantee Payments.*
- ☐ *Help with Meeting Redundancy Costs for Employers in Financial Difficulty.*
- ☐ *Offsetting Pensions against Redundancy Payments.*
- ☐ *Redundancy.*
- ☐ *Redundancy Consultation and Notification.*
- ☐ *The Redundancy Payments Scheme: A guide for employers, employees and others.*
- ☐ *Rules Governing Continuous Employment and a Week's Pay.*
- ☐ *The Transfer of an Undertaking.*

The Advisory Conciliation and Arbitration Service (ACAS)

ACAS provides a wide range of information on employment and industrial relations; the service is free and confidential – to know more, visit the ACAS website: www.acas.org.uk. Publications for purchase and free leaflets about ACAS services are available from ACAS Reader Ltd on 01455 852 225.

Lay-Offs and Short-Time Working. London, ACAS, 1996. An advisory leaflet.

Redundancy Handling. London, ACAS, 1996. An employer's handbook summarising the key elements in managing redundancy.

Incomes Data Services (IDS)

IDS has a series called *Employment Law Handbooks*; for more information, call Customer Services on 030 7324 2599 or visit the IDS website – www.incomesdata.co.uk.

Redundancy. Employment Law Handbook Series 2, No. 10. London, IDS, 1996. A comprehensive text covering both statute and case-law on all aspects of redundancy.

Transfer of Undertakings. Employment Law Handbook Series 2, No. 8. London, IDS, 1995. A largely legal text explaining the background and details of the TUPE regulations, including references to numerous tribunal and court cases.

Redundancy legislation

The principal statutes and regulations relating to redundancy are as follows:

- Employment Rights Act 1996: individual rights
  - definition of redundancy
  - entitlement to, and calculation of, redundancy payments
  - exclusions
  - unfair dismissal.
- Trade Union and Labour Relations (Consolidation) Act 1992 and Trade Union Reform and Employment Rights Act 1993: collective rights
  - definition of collective redundancy
  - trade unions' and employee representatives' rights to information and consultation.
- Transfer of Undertakings (Protection of Employment) Regulations 1981 and Collective Redundancies and Transfer of Undertakings (Protection of Employment) (Amendments) Regulations 1995
  - individual protection against redundancy and of contractual rights
  - collective consultation rights.

Other legislation that can have a bearing on redundancy includes all the anti-discrimination statutes: the Sex Discrimination Act 1975, Race Relations Act 1976, Disability Discrimination Act 1995.

Case-law

Readers wishing to study the legal aspects of redundancy in more detail, and particularly to follow developments in case-law, are advised to refer to the IPD publications listed above, and to consult the annual indexes of the monthly Industrial Relations Law Reports (IRLR) and IDS Briefs. Both these journals classify reported cases under various subject headings.

INDEX